Balance in Motion

Living in Natural Harmony with Parkinson's

TREVOR PRASAD

Copyright © 2025 by Trevor Prasad
1st Edition 2025
ISBN: 978-1-764 1837-5-8

All rights reserved.

No portion of this book may be reproduced in any form without written permission from the publisher or author, except as permitted by Australian copyright law.

NATRAOMI ® and the stylised logo of the Spiral Aloe Polyphylla are a registered Trade Mark.

For my granddaughter Aria Rose and all the other little ones that follow.

*Life is like riding a bicycle. To keep your balance,
you must keep moving.*

~ Albert Einstein, 1930

Contents

Foreword	VII
Author's Note	XI
Part 1 LIFE'S ADVENTURES	
1. At One...	3
2. An Unlikely Pack	15
3. The Evolutionary Step	21
4. A Window Into My Future	29
Part 2 EMPOWERING...	
5. Seek to Understand	43
6. Three Pillars	49
7. G.I.N.	83
8. Inspiring Others to Live in Natural Harmony	93
9. Finding Your Happiness	97
10. Wellness	105
Part 3 FOLLOW YOUR PASSIONS	
11. Adapting & Embracing Change	121
12. Balance & Precision	125
13. The Plot Thickens	131

14.	Carlo Abarth	139
15.	Music Is For Life	145
16.	Come Stai	151
17.	Going Solo	161
18.	Soar to New Heights	173
19.	In a Pickle	181
20.	The Evolving You	187

Nourish Yourself	193
"Intrigo dal Cielo Oscuro"	197
Stay Connected	201

Foreword

We all have our unique stories to tell. I've always been fascinated by the human condition and as a psychiatrist with nearly 50 years' experience, I've heard more stories than most.

Self-stories or stories we tell ourselves about ourselves derive from our upbringing, our peers, and from the society and culture to which we belong. For most of us, these derivative narratives see us through our daily experiences as we live our happy and fulfilled lives.

But when things go wrong in life, when there is trauma, an unexpected challenge, or physical illness, our stories may not be adequate to sustain us through trying times. It may become necessary to modify or rewrite our stories so that we can adapt to new and difficult circumstances.

Now, rewriting one's own story is not necessarily easy. It requires not only inner strength and determination, but also intelligence and an ability to objectify and examine one's own self-story. And most importantly, in order to become the master of one's own identity under duress, good emotional grounding and regulation are extremely helpful.

Human resilience, the capacity to withstand adversity and bounce back stronger, is a very valuable personal attribute, but it is not always there when you need it. Some of us do better than others in this regard depending on circumstances, personality and background.

From my own experience, I believe that we can all learn a lot from those who demonstrate resilience when needed.

And an excellent account of such a person is the story of my friend Trevor Prasad.

I've known Trevor for many years now. We met as hiking mates walking trails together around Australia, short and long, hard and easy. Trevor always impressed me, not only as a pragmatic individual who could fix things when they broke which has been a godsend to someone like me who is completely impractical, but also as a man with a vast wealth of knowledge about a wide range of interests and topics.

Trev is a fabulous dancer, a serious student of music, and a talented musician himself. His ability to glide around a dance floor sweeping beautiful women off their feet is enviable.

His love of motor sports has seen him enjoy numerous car club events on racetracks, riding powerful motor bikes across high mountain ranges on most of the world's continents, and as the owner of unique, beautiful and powerful machines.

Trevor and I have always shared a love of hiking as a way of experiencing the beauty and profundity of nature. Aesthetics means a lot to Trevor who adores being alone in nature, relishing the sights, sounds and smells of our beautiful earth. And in tandem with all of this is Trevor's deep absorption in spiritual matters.

Well-rounded is the best way to describe Trevor whose life before he became ill was by no means perfect, but it was full of adventure, romance and productive curiosity.

When he first realised, he was beset with a degenerative chronic illness, Trevor understandably was distressed. I remember camping with him by a beautiful waterway in the outback of the Northern Territory soon after his diagnosis had been confirmed. He was withdrawn and sulky which was not surprising. But that did not last long.

In the months and years that have followed, he has been without a doubt the perfect exemplar of what it means to be resilient.

Not only have I seen no evidence of a depressed mood on the many occasions we have been together since then, but Trevor has actively and methodically investigated his condition, the pros and the cons, of how to live his life under increasingly difficult circumstances. And most importantly, Trevor has used his own agency in deciding how he wants to have his condition managed. It was not only by the medical profession, but by dieticians, occupational therapists, psychologists, holistic healers, researchers and anyone else who is involved in the treatment of this insidious and disabling condition.

What has stood out is Trevor's independent and motivated approach. For a man with ever increasing restrictions, he has achieved remarkable things both physical and psychological.

The Buddha said that all life is suffering. Perhaps that is somewhat of an exaggeration, but it has a ring of truth about it. Life is full of challenges and the art of living is not about avoiding such difficulties but learning how to deal with them effectively.

To my mind that is exactly what Trevor has done not only with style and grace, courage and tenacity, but also with intelligence and panache.

I urge you to read his writings and savour the joy he himself continues to experience despite all his challenges.

Dr Nigel Strauss

Author's Note

Empowerment is the gift I would like to pass on as you develop your own thoughts and approach in living a positive, meaningful life, in harmony and balance with your chronic condition.

I will share my approach and key focus that has worked for me, while recognising I am not a medical practitioner. Rather, this is an account of my personal experiences and observations of my own symptom management. In addition to that, I include my own interpretations and subjective thoughts on how I have been able to reverse some symptoms and slow the onset while continuing to lead an adventurous life.

Wishing you much joy, and contentment in your life, as you expand your consciousness and personal journey of discovery.

Part 1

LIFE'S ADVENTURES

Chapter 1
At One...

4   BALANCE IN MOTION

With eyes fixated deep into the bend, left shoulder slightly dropped, you push forward on the left side of the handlebar to meet the apex of the lefthand corner. Gently, you allow the bike to settle into a lean as you shift your movement and attention towards the right apex to complete a beautiful set of esses. With pinpoint accuracy, you are now well placed to allow the bike to drift to the centreline while opening up to maximum throttle.

This counterintuitive art of **counter-steering,** once mastered, is the only safe method to corner at speed. It is totally intoxicating as you become **at one with machine**, effortlessly swaying from side to side with perfect precision through the twisties.

Two wheels are so elegant, providing pure harmony in motion.

In contrast, four wheels subject the occupants to constant pitching (left and right) with an ever present outward lean through the bends created by the g-force effect.

Having owned a number of scooters for the urban commute commencing with a 125 cc, then 250, followed by an Aprilia 500, and then BMW's 650 Sport, I was relatively late to big bikes.

In 2010, I graduated to a most beautifully balanced sports tourer, the R1200r. I called it the bi-plane of motorbikes (drawing comparisons to early planes that had the heads of the motor protruding out to the side with air cooling fins). The configuration of my 'boxer' motor (with the heads of the motor out either side) serves two purposes. First, it lowers the centre of gravity. Second, it contributes to the wonderful sense of balance and control (almost akin to a tight rope trapeze artist holding a balance beam).

It was two years prior to purchasing my first motorcycle (as opposed to scooters) that I got the 'adventure riding' bug. I ticked the box to rent an R1200RT in Barcelona, Spain, to join a small group for an 18-day tour. The R1200RT is BMW's full-fairing 'road tourer', capable of comfortably cruising autobahns at 250 kilometres per hour all day.

After a shake-down ride around the rugged Montserrat Mountains, we headed to the Port of Barcelona to board an overnight ship to the port of Civitavecchia, just north of Rome. Our bikes survived the crossing and we arrived into port later than expected. As dusk set in, we moved at a decent pace, taking about two and a half hours to reach the most well preserved historic fortified *Citadel* (old city centre) of San Gimignano. It was a most memorable evening ride. It was also a reminder to always keep a calm mind, observe your environment, and go with flow. I'll never forget as darkness fell, the incessant honking and flashing of lights as a black menacing Alfa Romeo Quadrifoglio came from behind creating his own third lane down the centre white line of a back-country road, splitting us and the oncoming traffic. By now, we certainly knew we had arrived in Italy. The Italians are awesome drivers, driving with passion and purpose.

Our *Tuscany and Provence* tour would take us through, Sienna, Firenze, Portofino, and Cinque Terra before heading through the French riviera. Heading inland through France's southern gorges and canyon country of the Verdon, we picked up the

Costa Brava coastline, and headed back to Barcelona to complete our loop.

I was hooked on adventure motorcycling after what had become my first of many overseas trips on two wheels, beyond the extensive touring at home in Australia.

Forgive me if I provide just a brief account of the following most memorable overseas motorcycle adventures.

My intent here is to set the scene of an adventurous life, but more importantly to demonstrate throughout this book that the quest for new experiences is a mindset you can continue to adopt, even after a health related diagnosis.

Maintaining an adventurous spirit, no matter what life circumstances may present for each and everyone of us.

The Essence of Morocco (and Beyond)

Morocco is a country where it is nice to have the luxury of a support crew given the pretty remote parts of the Sahara Desert we traversed, and with very little English spoken (Arabic and Amazigh/Berber are the official languages with French as a useful second). Having booked my Morocco group tour, I had also planned a solo trip through northern Spain during the week prior, and additional time to myself after Morocco to traverse the length of Portugal (before returning the motorbike back to Madrid).

So, I hatched a plan to take the long way down to Seville (the starting point of the Morocco tour). The first step was to pick up a rental bike from IMT Bike in Madrid. My now favoured steed of choice for the next 29 days (and subsequent adventures) was a GS1200R, BMW's all purpose adventure tourer. Commencing in a north-westerly direction to explore the historic old cities (ciudades históricas) of Ávila, Salamanca and Ciudad Rodrigo, before heading south through Plasencia, Cáceres, to Seville.
Before Ávila, the Aqueduct of Segovia is amongst the world's best preserved examples of a Roman aqueduct. I played with my camera to capture the imposing two-tiered 167 arches. This aqueduct was built in the first century AD as a means to channel water from nearby springs in the mountains to the township of Segovia. Speaking of Romans, it is interesting to learn that Ciudad Rodrigo was the most western end of the Roman empire.

For accommodation throughout Spain, I like to seek out the historic *Parador* guest houses. The word parador stems from the Spanish word parar, "to stop" (a place for travellers to rest). Today, a parador are hotel-style accommodation that are typically in UNESCO heritage listed buildings including former monasteries and castles. One of my most favourite cultural experiences was staying at a parador in Ávila.

On to Morocco, crossing the Strait of Gibraltar with our motorbikes under the guidance of our experienced tour operators Iberian Motorcycle Tours (IMT Bike), we took the option of a ferry from Algeciras to Ceuta. Although Ceuta is on the northern tip of the African continent, it has remained under political control of Spain since the 17th century.

We ventured off on our loop around Morocco through Chefchaouen, Fez, over the Atlas Mountains to Erfoud, the orange sands of Merzouga, Quarzazate, before heading back up north through Marrakech and Rabat. The landscape changes immensely from the fertile green of the north to the arid desert of the south, dissected by the Atlas Mountain range.

Visiting Fez was like being on a *Monty Python's, Life of Brian* film set. Your personal space is invaded as you compete to walk down the bustling narrow streets of the *medina* (old city). Just roll the cameras and immerse yourself straight back into biblical times. With the cries of "Balak, Balak..." you learn quickly to get out of the way of the mules and heavily ladened donkey carts carrying sacks of produce, sacks of building materials, and unreasonably wide loads, rendering them unstoppable.

The vibrancy of the souks, the marketplaces that still very much serve the needs of the locals. They offer an array of fragrant spices neatly arranged in triangular mounds, carcasses of meats hanging in the breeze of the open air and unrefrigerated butcheries. The latter provides the sight of trays of *offal* that are now confronting to westerners who have become so unaccustomed as to the importance and nutritional value in eating liver, heart, kidneys, stomach, brains, and tongue.

It was a totally surreal experience to step through a doorway from all the mayhem and noise of the medina, to shut the door and find ourselves in total tranquility of our *riad* – surrounded by the beauty of Moroccan architectural elements of: the ornate carved woodwork; the intricate, geometric, hand-chiseled *Zellige* tilework; and the smooth, seamless, water-resistant finish of *Tadelakt* plaster. Riads are the inward-facing courtyard homes that provided a sanctuary from the harsh elements, security, and protection for the families of nobility and wealthy merchants.

At street level of our riad was a pharmacy combining traditional and modern day remedies. Fes historically has been a centre for education and knowledge. The traditional herbalists, *Attār*, are renowned for their preparations to not only relieve physical ailments but for emotional and spiritual healing. Regardless of beliefs, it was inspiring to see the blend of traditional remedies provided by the *Attār's* combined with a modern day approach of the *Saydali* (the name in Arabic given to western pharmacists).

The Atacama Desert through Chile, Bolivia, and Peru

Primarily running through the north of Chile for over 1,000 kilometres is the Atacama Desert, flanked by the Chilean Coast Range and the Andes Mountains (and partly extends across the border of Bolivia).

As we leave the long white sands of the northern coastal town of Iquique, within half an hour we had wound ourselves up and onto the plateau of the Atacama Desert. At an altitude of 3,500 metres, this would become our average altitude for the next 16 days.

Looking upon earth, you'll observe the extensive white blob over the southwest corner of Bolivia that is The Solar de Uyuni. This is the largest salt pan in the world at 10,582 square kilometres. It is heavily policed to minimise illegal trafficking. However, organised tours are possible including a stay at a hotel made out of salt blocks. Although we didn't ride onto the salt pan as such, you could well imagine the surrounding landscape we had to traverse over the preceding two days to get to the isolated town of Uyuni (on the edge of the solar). Mud flats of dark brown encrusted in salt, it was easy to be lulled into a false sense of security, pretending to be Donald Campbell (1960s Bonneville Salt Flats in Utah) attempting to break the land speed record.

The timing of our trip was critical as only six weeks earlier this route was not passable. The wet season turns this whole region into a mud bog. It had supposedly dried out for us to cross from the Bolivian border to Uyuni. Our party of a lead rider and 11 guests, and a Dodge RAM all-wheel-drive support vehicle, had started to spread out. Stopping frequently for photos, I was now mid pack. As I cranked up the pace, fixated on the bunch ahead, all of a sudden I could see a mass of swerve lines carved out of the chocolate brown earth from the bikes ahead of me who had broken through the white salt crust. I could see that there was a depression that I presumed had created the soft spot (with a natural water course underneath). I washed off half my speed as I swung to the left to find fresh (hopefully more stable) salt. I'm now approximately at 60 kilometres per hour. As it became evident I wouldn't be able to completely avoid the bog, now came the unsettling but required technique of, moving your butt as far back on the saddle (to change the centre of gravity) and accelerate in a bid to keep the nose up, and lighten the load on the front wheel. One of our fellow riders took a more conservative approach and slowed to a point where his front wheel ended up being buried above the axle line with the rider going for a gentle (thankfully unscathed) tumble over the handlebars with the sudden stop. Four of us spent the best part of an hour digging the bike out, clearing the thick sticky mud, and ensuring the bike was still operational.

There is a whole other book on this adventure alone, with experiences that included hiring a dedicated scramble bike in La Paz to do a loop of the infamous Death Road Bolivia. The highlight of this tour was our finale at Cusco in Peru, riding out to Machu Picchu where we soaked up the culture and beauty of the 15th-century "Lost City of the Incas" and the Inca Empire.

While in Peru, wandering through the back laneways of Cusco, I struck up a spiritually enlightening conversation with a *shaman.* The Peru shamans are a group of Andean medicine men/women applying ancient Inca knowledge and wisdom to take people on a transformational journey of self-discovery and healing. I so much wanted to experience the medicinal plant Ayahuasca that the shamans use to help connect mind, body, and spirit, but I was out of time having booked a side excursion to stay in a remote village on the Amazon river (south of Iquitos).

Barcelona, Sardinia, Marseille, Italy, Austrian & Swiss Alps, France, and Barcelona

The importance of 2017 will become more clear as you read on. Nevertheless, I am forever grateful to have had this most epic 32-day self guided adventure through Europe on two wheels.

The Giro d'Italia was about to start on the following day that our ship (with motorcycle) arrived at the Port of Alghero, in Sardinia, where we were pleasantly rewarded with a full dry-rehearsal of the Giro d'Italia opening ceremony. There are too many stories to relay here, but I do look back very fondly at *il mio giro di 10 giorni* (my own 10 day tour) around Sardinia. I was keen to gleam some understanding as to why Sardinia is regarded as one of the blue zone regions of the world (where inhabitants live significantly longer and healthier lives). I probably need to go back and spend significant time in Nuoro province (and brush up on my Italian) to even hope to start to appreciate the cultural nuances. However, within moments of arriving on the island, it was easy to get drawn in to the sense of calm and chilled lifestyle. There is no question we sampled some beautiful mediterranean food and plenty of Omega-3 through a diet of fish most nights. It was heartwarming to see how the locals interacted with one another and guests, with their sense of balance and harmony towards themselves as a community and family while co-existing within the harsh environment of this island.

Throughout my adventures on two wheels, my key learnings are:

- Allow yourself to slow down and fully immerse yourself in the experience.

- Take time to engage with people, place and culture – what can we learn from each other.

- Be impulsive, seize opportunities to try something different, something unexpected.

- Go with the flow, there is no wrong decision.

- It's ok to throw yourself in the deep-end.

With respect to your motorcycle riding – have confidence in the skill and knowledge you have acquired, trust in your abilities while applying common sense.

Riding a 259 kilogram (571 pound) bike (plus rider/passenger and luggage), is not about strength, and nor should one be overly concerned about the adrenaline inducing power.
It is all about being *at one*, developing the finesse, and balance, while respectfully twisting the wrist to protect your passenger, yourself and machine – and ride with full commitment, without fear, or guilt.

> In the zone, your mind will find calm and stillness, as you experience the wonderful meditative qualities of riding – settling into a state of ***harmony in motion.***

Motorcycling truly declutters your mind as you let go of the extraneous noise in your life and become singularly focused on the task at hand.

Beyond two wheels, we will explore finding your balance and harmony in life.

Maintaining an adventurous spirit.

Enjoying life's ride!

# Chapter 2
An Unlikely Pack

As we squashed five rather tall, exuberant hikers into a mid-sized SUV with the smallest in the middle (that would be me) expectations where high as we set forth for Lake Tali Karng in Eastern Victoria.

It became abundantly clear how diverse we all were as the philosophical pondering questioned the notion of "How would we know if we were happy?" By the time we arrived at our campsite we were all in a state of euphoria nonetheless. The scene was set for an interesting weekend of exploration, metaphysically, spiritually, and well beyond the physical aspects of hiking.

What was assured was the formation of an eclectic group of ultimately eight hikers. If it wasn't so true, it sounds like a corny riddle, but the team (the importance of which will make sense later) comprised of two chiropractors, two psychiatrists, two lawyers, an IT professional, and an agriculturalist.

We dubbed ourselves the 'ANZAC Day Gourmet Campers'. We took it in turns to present the evening meal for the group. I don't think we were trying to outdo each other per se. It was more that no one wanted to let the team down. I had worked out that I could freeze a preprepared meatloaf that would defrost during the first day hike. The meatloaf was well received and complemented the cache of fine bottles of red that became a feature for our hikes. (We eventually got wiser and realised it was better to decant wine into wine bladders rather than lugging bottles.)

AN UNLIKELY PACK

There were wild ideas of hunting a kangaroo Bear Grylls style (with nothing more than a Gerber knife). Accordingly, there was much delight when one of the lads produced some succulent kangaroo fillets. Cryovac fillets of course, but nonetheless true to his word. We got to indulge in a feast of 'roo in red-wine jus.

Collaboration and sharing the load were a key theme. Too much amusement for our wives and girlfriends, accommodation involved the sharing of a six-person old style canvas tent. Our instigator of many of these hikes is a fun loving German who cares very much about the team and keeping every one together.
The sections of our monolithic tent were expertly divided up. With looks of concern when I revealed the hiking pack that I had brought, that looked more like it belonged on a British television set for the sitcom "It Ain't Half Hot Mum" set in the era of WW2. There where sighs of relief when they could see this style of pack was designed to strap gear on the outside and thus carry ones fair share of the load. I had passed my initiation!

My pack was soon dubbed the **Tardis**. *Doctor Who fans will relate to what I'm referring to. The Tardis Time Machine expanded inside, disproportionately to the British Telephone box exterior.*

Updating technology and gear became an obsession with a dose of healthy competitiveness as to who had the next new gadget for each ensuing expedition. I might have been amongst the first to break away from the main tent by acquiring a one person tent. Rather than being ridiculed, one person tents became the standard as we all revelled in the luxury of having our own space. We all have accumulated different tents to cater for the differing weather conditions and duration of hike.

18   BALANCE IN MOTION

The route into Tali Karng follows the Wellington River upstream for 17 kilometres, crossing the river 16 times. By the time you have pulled off your boots and peeled off your socks to wade through the often treacherous crossings, your mind became consumed with how to get smarter and more efficient with gear. Martin had arrived earlier at the campsite. I'll never forget the most hilarious moment when an exhausted Ben called out to Martin (who was taking an early bath) for a piggy-back across the final crossing. "I'll throw you my pack". "Nah, leave it on", came the reply from 6'4" Martin of German stock as he waded bare across the river stones. Martin proceeded to carry 90 kilograms of Ben (still strapped to his 32-kilogram pack) to safe ground with perfect balance and sure-footedness. The vision is forever etched. ;-/

My solution was to invest in some German-made Lowe hike boots that have a wonderful quick release lace system comprising of loops and eyelets with smooth-action bearings. River crossings where no longer tedious. The boots literally fell off your feet once released. The bearing system ensured the laces self adjust and fasten easily. This also ensured that you didn't get hotspots or pressure points on the upper arch of your feet.

Expedition planning is definitely half the fun. Being resourceful, getting creative, thinking through contingencies, and having the confidence in the knowledge that you are well prepared to the best that can be expected.

However, the real knack is to then let go - accept that you have done your best and go with the flow.

To not fall into the trap of overthinking.

To not overly obsess as to whether you have thought through everything.

True confidence comes from being resilient and maintaining a balanced outlook while embracing the unexpected eventualities.

You are resourceful. You will find your path.

Chapter 3
The Evolutionary Step

Larapinta

All our hikes have had there own unique elements. However, there is no question that the mid section of the Larapinta Trail, West MacDonnell Ranges in the Northern Territory, created another level of preparation and a maturing of the group. There are 12 sections of the Larapinta starting from Alice Springs to the most western end at Mt Sonder. Spanning 223 kilometres, it is suggested that it will take 12 to 15 days to complete the entire trail.
Our first expedition to Larapinta was to tackle the toughest mid section from Stanley Chasm to Ellery Creek.

By far, our most gruelling day was the last section from Hugh Gorge to Ellery Creek (south). It was a challenging 33.6 kilometres. This section was made all the more demanding by soaring temperatures of 38 degrees celsius which required us to start the day with carrying 9 kilograms of water. Making an earlier start at 6:00 am in a bid to escape the heat proved futile. We traversed open country between two ridge lines. I'd packed enough hydrolite for the team. However, by the time we descended the saddle, I had pretty much exhausted my water with the remaining 4 kilometres to go. It had been an 11.5-hour day arriving at camp around 5:30 pm feeling reasonably dehydrated.

The most awe inspiring aspect of the Larapinta (apart from being in the middle of nowhere in central Australia) are these ridge lines. If you can think of an aerial photo of the world oceans you will see ridges formed on the seabed. It is hard to comprehend that the ridge lines we were now walking on were once the ocean floor from an inland sea that existed during the Cretaceous period (144 to 65 million years ago) and stretched over one quarter of the current Australian continent. Australia is such an ancient land!

Speaking of ancient, as you meander through gorges, gullies, and river edges you will encounter the magnificent *Macrosamia MacDonnellii* (a cycad palm with large frond-like, pinnate bluish-green leaves). These are only found within 200 kilometres east and west of Alice Springs in central Australia. It was once thought that these cycads contained the same genus that stem from the plants that were munched on by dinosaurs of the Jurassic period 30 million years ago. However, in 2012, researchers at the University of Queensland, the Queensland Herbarium, and The Australian National University proposed the cycads were in fact a mere 10 to 20 million years old. Either way, we are talking ancient history that continues to evolve.

> *It is interesting to see the accelerated rate of genetic sequencing in many areas of science. That is challenging previously conceived ideas.*

We all came away form Larapinta for ever changed from the enormity of the experience.

Mount Anne

Hiking really is a mental game. It is so important to have confidence in your abilities, invest in the right equipment, and trust in your gear.

Day 1 was the slowest pace I'd ever experienced. With an average pace of 1 kilometre per hour, we picked yourselves over *car-sized* granite boulders with gaping crevices in between. To slip would almost certainly result in serious leg injuries. This is where reliance on your gear becomes so important. I've always been a proponent of hike poles (which by now everyone in our group had adopted). It is amazing how you can wedge the titanium tip of your poles into the most minute crack, seam, or divot, providing a far greater level of sure-footedness, balance, and control.

Back to Larapinta for a brief moment as an example of using hike poles to an advantage. Between Birthday Waterhole and Hugh Gorge, we encountered an extremely steep 15-metre descent off the spine of the Razorback Ridge, comprising of very loose shale rock. Those without poles will face the slope opting to go down backwards on hands and knees. Having poles provides enough confidence to maintain your stance and slowly walk down in a normal forward facing direction, with your poles effectively acting as a hand rail.

As I opened the tent fly to inspect the sunrise, I was warmly greeted by a blanket of cloud rolling up the valley almost quite literally into my tent. We were at just over 1,000 metres with the cloud obscuring what was a deathly drop-off only metres from my tent. We had arrived late into camp and had not fully oriented ourselves. It was partly because of the distraction and beauty of Mount Anne summit, but mostly because we were racing the setting sun to secure our tent on the solid rock plateau below Mount Anne summit.

To be at one with the environment is so grounding. The experiences is so surreal and totally humbling when you realise how small and insignificant we are in this vast landscape.

I have this overwhelming belief that if you trust in your senses, walk lightly on this planet, be truly at one with your surrounds, take the time to mindfully observe, and to not fight against the environment, you will witness *harmony in motion* as mother nature will guide you.

A key feature of Mount Anne is having to traverse the infamous and treacherous 'Notch'. Notably, a seven-metre high free climb. It can be achieved by sandwiching yourself between a seam and scrambling onto a shelf (known as The Notch) before scaling a further three metres to safety. The shelf has a rakish angle of approximately 15 degrees which would be rather interesting in the wet.

Before you swing yourself up onto the shelf, you have to stand on a foothold that is barely half of one boot in depth.
You really only have one shot at swinging yourself up onto the angled shelf and finding a hand hold. To miss the hand hold is to slide off the shelf with little chance of maintaining balance (regardless of whether you miraculously find the half boot foothold).

To be a lead climber, it is better to be over six feet as you need to be able to get a finger hold on the back seam of the Notch. If you are under six feet, there is a technique where you can use an ice axe. The handle length of the ice axe will extend your reach sufficiently to allow the axe head to be wedged into the required seam. We have a few tall lads at our disposal. Martin is the most agile and always up for a challenge.

The lead climber secures a 15-metre rope for both hauling up the packs, but more importantly acting as a safety line (belay) for the rest of the team. This is where a *Munter Hitch* can help.

> ***The Munter Hitch*** *named after the Swiss mountaineer, Werner Munter in the 70s, who popularised what was also known as the 'Italian Hitch'.*
> *This hitch is known as a flip-flop knot that is used with a carabiner to create a belay system. A belay is used by climbers and rescuers to control the friction of a rope to enable, someone to be lowered safely, or to maintain tension and support for a fellow climber to ascend.*

As the unofficial technical/safety officer, I went to a local climbing shop to purchase a climbing sling (a weight-bearing nylon webbing in a continuous loop, 16 millimetres wide), and chose the 120-centimetre loop, and a new carabiner. With these items, you can create a light-weight emergency harness.

- Crossing the sling, you put the sling behind a person's upper back. Putting their arms through the looped ends created and bringing both looped ends together in front to snap them together with a carabiner. You then attach your rope to the carabiner using a Munter hitch and thereby creating a very quick and easy belay system (to safely guide your fellow hikers up and over the Notch).

If Larapinta was tough, Mount Anne had exceeded the groups prior experience.

After all, we were a bunch of hikers punching above our weight. We were not mountaineers!

Take your time to navigate through obstacles. You will get through.

Chapter 4

A Window Into My Future

As I walked out of the neurologist's office accompanied by my dear friend Lina, I thought to myself "Well, that's interesting. That is a window into my future".

My father was a GP, and my mother a nurse. However, the subliminal effects of growing up in a medical family didn't quite prepare me for the diagnosis I'd just been given beyond a very basic understanding of this chronic illness.

Now back to my hike friend's for a moment, and the relevancy of at least four of them with medical training will now become clear. There had been a few general comments on a hike during 2017, that "Hey Trev, it might be good for you to see a neurologist". If I think back then I was more bemused rather than especially resistant. But, my friends where observing things that were not quite apparent to me.

In fact, once you become aware of this condition, there are a bunch of symptoms you can reliably look back on as early markers. The challenge is that in isolation, it is not reasonable to assume any of these early symptoms will translate to a chronic illness.

I will dwell on this point briefly, as I believe that it is so important to not jump to conclusions with "They should have told me. Why didn't they pick that up earlier?", and other such thoughts.

It is natural to want to seek answers. The medical term for no known cause is *idiopathic*. There is much concerted research efforts around toxicity of our environments and food chain, to better understand the role of genetics, and much advancements in factors such as gut microbiome. Sometimes, it is just what it is. I have found it better to accept and focus on informing myself on what steps I can take to minimise the onset while getting on with living life.

It can be hard to stay calm and objective. I have found it really important to be kind to yourself and allow every emotion to be fully expressed.

> ***Notions of 'why is this happening to me, this is so unfair' are words that never preoccupy my thoughts.***

"Raise your left hand and make circular motions with your index finger", came the words from the neurologist as he held my relaxed right arm and proceeded to gently move my wrist up and down.

"Hmmm, yes you have 'ratchet wrist'. As soon as he uttered those words I could totally sense and understand the analogy. My wrist was not smooth in its action (when presented with a neurological challenge created by the circular motion of my left hand), and indeed my right wrist was like a ratchet moving through multiple splines.

As I walked across the room "You have cogwheel gait rigidity in your right leg". This is what my hike buddies had picked up on but was less obvious as an issue for me at the time.

It was a couple of years post diagnosis that while riding my bike, it felt like my chain was skipping when in fact it was my right leg not moving freely in a circular motion, unable to provide the required even and consistent pressure on the pedal.

"Did you know your right arm doesn't swing when you walk?" I was curious by this as I had a vague realisation, but thought that was just me. I can't quite pinpoint when my lack of swing was any different, but it is certainly an example of a symptom I'd had for several decades.

My right hand tremor started to become more prevalent which was the key driver in my seeking a neurologists opinion.

"We now have a definitive diagnoses", came the caring words. "I am sorry to inform you, you have early-onset Parkinson's, further categorised by a tremor dominant, RH".

My overwhelming reaction was that I had walked into these consulting room and I was certainly going to walk out of them. Retrospectively, I was very naive. I thought this was something for when I was of old age.

"There is no disease-modifying drug" (no cure) for Parkinson's.

As Lina and I drove away from the consulting rooms we lamented over songs like *Shake Rattle and Roll*. (OK, I'm giving away my generation, but Bill Haley & The Comets had released this hit single in 1960).

Perhaps appropriately I was born in 1964 towards the end of the rock 'n roll era. Many might know the tune *For Goodness Sake, I've got the Hippy Hippy Shakes* (recorded by the young 17 year old American artist Chan Romero in 1959).

I find that music and humour helps.

What really matters is finding an approach that works best for you in terms of maintaining a healthy perspective. Adopting a wonderful sense of balance and objectivity towards the meaningful life, you can continue to create for yourself today.

Morocco

Atacama Desert, Bolivia

Atacama Desert, Chile, Bolivia, Peru, Amazon River

European Motorcycle Adventure

LARAPINTA TRAIL, WEST MACDONNELL RANGES, NT.

LARAPINTA TRAIL, WEST MACDONNELL RANGES, NT.

Mount Anne, Tasmania.

Part 2

POSITIVELY QUESTIONING…
EMPOWERING…

Chapter 5
Seek to Understand

The intent of this chapter is to provide a quick reference that might be useful to revisit whenever you might be experiencing a degree of frustration, or a degree of confusion, through seemingly conflicting advice.

These are some of my guiding principles and approach I like to remind myself of in all human interactions and in overcoming ingrained response mechanisms.

Don't judge, seek to understand. These are the gentle words etched in my subconscious.

Everyone has their own very unique set of experiences that have shaped the very essence of who we all have become. Tolerance is one of my most treasured values.

A person's perspective is valid and real for them.

Should the focus ever be on who is right or who is wrong. After all, I might be wrong. I have evolved to no longer need to convince others of my views.

Part of self-realisation is to be confident and content with who we are, devoid of external drivers. Once we arrive at this point, we are able to pause and understand others with empathy. We are no longer in conflict with the world and others will be drawn to you. If you try to follow this ethos, please be careful not to judge yourself if on occasion, you momentarily digress. Be kind to yourself. Allow yourself to be human. We are not on this planet to be perfect.

To take the time to truely hear and acknowledge another, for me is a higher virtue.

One of my jazz mentors introduced me to the concept of Dadirri, a cultural practice of our First Nation people. It is a form of deep contemplative listening. With elements of meditation and mindfulness, the Aborigines have a deep connection to land, people, and spirit. You might relate to other indigenous cultures. I think modern society can learn a lot from ancient civilisations. It is fascinating to think that the Aboriginal people are known to have occupied mainland Australia for more than 65,000 years (predating modern human settlement of Europe and the Americas). In a council (corroboree) of Aboriginal elders the emphasis and importance is on being heard, rather than agreeing on an outcome.

Having spent a couple of decades in corporate IT, my core skill was translating business requirements into the technical world. I became very attuned in observing and understanding people's differing points of view. What are the different business and more importantly personal drivers? A corporate executive will have a very different lens to a mid-level manager tasked with rolling out an initiative, to an end-user interacting with a system on a daily basis.

Organisations may differ but human nature is the same the world over.

The medical profession is no different. We are all products of our time and our exposure to education. Hence we are influenced by geopolitical and social environments. As a consequence, we are also shaped by global issues and events. It is also human nature whether it be at an individual level, organisational, or for health authorities and governments to take comfort and be swayed by 'group think'. People and organisations are drawn towards a common ideology.

I started adopting the following words as a reminder to *empower* myself as I embarked on a quest to further my understanding.

Empowering | Positively Questioning | Restorative

To not get frustrated when presented with seemingly conflicting advice and opinion. Rather, I believe it is more constructive to take the approach of ***positively questioning***. This is especially important when we recognise that there are no easy answers and no cure for many chronic neurological conditions.

Pursue your inner balance with compassion. Imagine how challenging it must be to work in a field where there is no clear solution for your patients. Be kind to yourself. Be kind to everyone else around you. If for no other reason, your cortisol level demands a state of calm and objectivity *(I will go into more detail on cortisol later)*.

For me, it has been more important to focus on what I can do for myself rather than be the passive observer. Thinking through the *restorative* aspects that I can do has provided a sense of control and achievement in minimising and slowing down the onset of my Parkinson's. In some instances, I have reversed a few symptoms. I do emphasise that I have enough core symptoms to remind me that this annoying Parkinson's thing ain't going away anytime soon.

Wishing you all the best as you seek to understand what positive steps you can take.

Connect with your resilient self and uncover a renewed approach.

You will find your buoyancy.

Chapter 6
Three Pillars

When asked as to how I manage my symptoms, my first response is always with *exercise, nutrition,* and *mindfulness.*

So, let's have fun breaking down these elements in detail throughout this chapter. The quick snapshot is:

- I soon got to learn that not all *exercise* is considered equal and that there is a very real need to have a multipronged approach.

- *Nutrition* is such an evolving space. I will share my approach and key focus that has worked for me while recognising that I am not a medical practitioner. Rather, this is an account of my personal experiences and observations of my own symptom management. I will also relate my own interpretations on how I have been able to reverse some symptoms and my subjective thoughts on slowing the onset of Parkinson's.

- *Mindfulness* is a higher state of consciousness that consumes your every waking thought. I will spend time on this topic as we discuss the idea of impermanence and embracing change while enjoying an active and meaningful life.

  As an aside, I used to say 'meditation' instead of *mindfulness.* I adjusted my thinking as I recognised that meditation is more of a subset of mindfulness. Meditation implies a conscious awareness (consciously allowing dedicated time to engage in a meditative practice).

Keep evolving. It is okay to adjust and refine your thinking.

Life is not static.

Exercise

And the Professionals on Your Team

"Scrunch the scarf into your right hand. With vigour, throw it to the ceiling followed by catching it with purpose while rapidly bringing your hand to your side. Now repeat each side six times".

I walked back across the room in front of 25+ health professionals who were here on a training program being delivered by my neurological physiotherapist, Marize. They were here to witness the improvements in movement achieved through an innovative approach to 'Parkinson's-specific' exercise.

Immediately following this singular but purposeful exercise, my walking gait (stride length, stability, smoothness of action, heel strike, and hip alignment) and pace was significantly improved.

Melissa McConaghy is a well regarded neurological physiotherapist based in Sydney. Together with her colleague Lynn Tullock, Melissa developed the *PD Warrior* exercise program. Over a two-year period, they researched, modelled, and tested the latest scientific evidence-based thinking on neuroplasticity and exercise. The challenge they were overcoming was that most health professionals generally agreed that exercise was good. However, there was little guidance to patients as to what forms of exercise are appropriate.

As you build out your own exercise regime, it is important to consider the differing benefits achieved through strength training, neurological exercises, and maintaining flexibility and agility, versus exercise for the pure joy and wellness factor such as walking your dog, cycling, and other regular group activities.

Neurological Physiotherapy

Neurological exercises are crucial in maintaining neuroplasticity and forming new neurological connections. There is scientific evidence that exercise can significantly improve symptoms while slowing down the progression of Parkinson's.

Your *neurological physiotherapist* is best placed to help you and ideally will incorporate the PD Warrior style of exercises. Melissa's PD Warrior book titled *The New Parkinson's Treatment-Exercise is Medicine* includes a 10-week challenge so that you can measure and experience the benefits. For further details, visit https://pdwarrior.com/

Physiotherapy

A regular *Physiotherapist* has the potential to be one of the most important practitioners (especially if you have had consultations prior to diagnosis). They will have the history and hands on approach to be able to observe and provide valuable input into changes in muscle quality and range of motion. Try and track down a physiotherapist that you may have seen within the last 5 to 10-year period prior to diagnosis. It could be quite a positive revelation.

I have consulted my physiotherapist Allan off and on for almost 20 years (13 years prior to diagnosis). When I told Allan of my di-

agnosis, with great enthusiasm and genuine curiosity, he flicked through my patient records (handwritten DL cards). With head nodding followed by lots of "Ahh's,... Oh yes,... and here again. Ah, it all makes sense!"
The penny had dropped for both of us as he joined the dots with years of unexplained (and recurring) tension around my upper thoracic spine. My often "stove pipe" rigidity in my legs. Almost with glee Allan will say "OK, let's dig some concrete out". Allan is highly skilled in *dry-needling* which for me works wonders as he finds knots. Knots that are trigger points where areas of muscle contract and hold tension. Dry-needling has been especially useful in releasing my upper glute/hip area, my hamstrings, and calfs.

For many of us with Parkinson's, we find it difficult to navigate tight spaces, negotiate bends with constant freezing (or micro freezing in my case), and falling (or catching a potential fall as I do daily).
I think I am lucking in that I don't really technically fall. Partly because I'm quite lean and agile (my body weight has been a constant c. 61 kilograms over the past five years). I have also maintained good strength. However, and by example, when I round the corner to head to my bathroom, I will often catch myself as I fall towards the door jam.

I navigate the lounge room by "furniture surfing", almost 'parkour' style as I go from couch, swivel chair, bookshelf, and table.

I recall one hilarious moment when I put my hand on the high-back of my Danish leather winged swivel chair, and promptly lost my balance. All I could do was slump myself into the chair which proceeded to spin me around. As the chair spun in the direction of my bedroom door, with sheer will power I leapt out and proceeded to do a shoulder roll onto the bed, laughing the whole time as I felt like I had just stared in my own Evel Kinevel Pin Ball Wizard game (only I was the pinball).

As I have a galley-style kitchen, you would think it would be relatively easy to take two side steps from my fridge to my sink. Having something in my hands routinely confuses my neurons and my legs decide to freeze as I grab and hang at a rakish angle by the sink edge, willing my legs to come join the party and get back underneath me where they belong.

Needless to say, after all these daredevil stunt activities it becomes rather worthwhile having a physiotherapist who can untangle the pulled and strained muscles. I always welcome a spot of dry needling to straighten me out.

"The closest I get to truly falling is a technique I have developed where I gently drop to one knee, with hands placed either side in a stance reminiscent of the Marvel action hero Thor, as I then proceed (metaphorically) to pick up my Mjölnir (hammer)".

Exercise Physiology

Exercise physiology (EP) was a new term to me. I soon got to learn the importance of having an EP on your team. While it becomes increasingly important to maintain physical strength to provide better stability and help minimise falls, the nature of Parkinson's (and other chronic illnesses) requires a very tailored approach.

My upper thoracic spine is like a wash board with each vertebrae not segmenting and rotating as freely as it should. My right leg has what is referred to as *cogwheel-gait rigidity* which compromises my walking gait. The effect of these symptoms translates to compensatory biomechanical issues. Hence, I tend to be quad dominant when I walk with my calfs getting more of a workout. My hip flexors are overloaded, with my upper glutes carrying tension.

Your exercise physiologist is trained to provide programs that form part of your treatment of your chronic illness, management of symptoms, preventative measures, and rehabilitation. (A *clinical exercise physiologist* will have a Master's degree and experience in practical clinical placements in a hospital, rehab, or related clinical environment).

You might like to have a look at the global organisation Kieser that was founded in Switzerland in 1967 providing an innovate approach to exercise and rehabilitation.
I am enjoying having access to highly specialised machines that can isolate specific muscle groups to increase strength and maintain neuroplasticity.

For those of us losing our fine motor skills in our hands, this impedes many daily tasks. By example, our ability to cut a loaf of bread, peel and dice vegetables, to shave, or manually brush my teeth, to write and type. My mouse hand routinely goes AWOL – combine this with my trigger finger and we have the potential for online shopping to be very expensive, LOL! For my regular Tuesday night chicken parma at my local pub, the staff add the note "Trevor's special" so that the chef knows to cut up my chicken into finger sized pieces. Other practical steps include installing a Toto Washlet bidet toilet.

Pilates

Osteopath or physiotherapist led pilates:
If we were to look at a Venn diagram (a set of interlocking shapes) it would illustrate that there is often a degree of overlap amongst the health professionals you consult with. I have found that having a differing angle and approach is very important. I have particularly valued using a *pilates reformer* which has been great in maintaining overall flexibility, upper arm strength, and in particular core strength. My osteopath also happens to do an annual *full body assessment* that looks at a number of measures such as muscle quality, strength, BMI (body mass index), flexibility, and range of motion. Your resulting data is then overlaid with the general populous to determine a number of indicators including your biological age.
If it weren't for this annoying Parkinson's, I am otherwise in great shape at age 60 with a biological age of 45. It is useful to obtain as much baseline data as practical so that you and your health professionals can monitor change.

Podiatry

Perhaps, under the guise of obtaining baseline data, I have found it useful to consult a *podiatrist*. It is common in Parkinson's for people to develop *foot-drop*. It is a loss of sensory feeling in the feet which compounds a person's walking gait and contributes to a heightened risk of falling.

Interestingly, early on in my diagnosis I was experiencing mild foot-drop (RF). Surprisingly, this is an example of a symptom I have been able to reverse. It is hard to isolate why I have achieved this, but it is likely to be a combination of my approach to exercise, nutrition, and mindfulness.

Well beyond the nice luxury of having my toe nails cut, your podiatrist is highly skilled in understanding the biomechanics of the body and at assessing change. Not so long ago, I had a situation where I had fluid retention (swelling) of my feet. My podiatrist was able to readily use an ultra-sound and rule out any vascular issues. With my tendency to be front-foot biased (as an outcome of my *festination),* we have conversations about postural alignment and focusing on correct heal-strike to improve gait. I routinely have calluses trimmed from my big toes. (Festination is characterised by a 'compromised centre of gravity' resulting in a forward stoop).

I have found it essential to be in zero-drop (totally flat) shoes. The moment I have even the slightest heel I find that it throws me forward enough to exacerbate my festination. Please be aware that while sneakers have a flat sole, most will have a built-in wedge creating a drop from heel to toe.

With shared knowledge, enthusiasm, and collaboration, it is good to see my podiatrist ditched his iconic Australian cattleman's elastic-sided boots in favour of 'barefoot-running style' shoes. He now looks more appropriately like an inner Melbourne hipster rather than a wealthy western grazier (cattle ranch owner). More importantly, his feet are thankful.

Reflexology

"You need to go see Papa", insisted Maitreya. I met Maitreya during one of my trips to Ubud in the mountains of central Bali. Long before westerners came, Ubud is steeped in history as a very sacred and spiritual place. Maitreya is the real-deal from India and comes from a strong linage of spiritual healers. If he says go to papa, then papa I will. An aspect of Parkinson's for most is experiencing a diminishing sensory perception in our feet. Papa happens to be one of the many talented and prolific painters in Bali. However, it was his proficiency in another art form that was the reason behind why I was sent.

Papa now in his late 80s is also a renowned *reflexologist*. Or you might also say torturer. With a wonderful smile and laughter, our chain-smoking Papa inflicts pain with almost sheer delight. Cigarette in one hand, alternating a selection of wooden paddles in the other, he pokes, twists between toes, and works on pressure points on your feet. It won't be for everyone's liking. I can nonetheless attest to the improved blood flow, foot sensory and reduced swelling of feet.

In the 1800s the Balinese art movement was influenced by the Dutch. Of particular note is also the German painter Walter Spiers (1895-1942). When in Ubud, I highly recommend that you visit the ARMA (Arunga Rai Museum of Art) to fully immerse yourself in the art history of Bali, especially the traditional pigments used, the warm earthy tones, and the meticulous detail.

Yoga

Yoga in the Western world has almost became a blood sport delivered by highly athletic 'energiser bunnies'. Now, I am deliberately exaggerating to illustrate a point. When in Asia, however, you will have a greater opportunity to experience the authentic *Indian Yogi* forms that are all about calming the sympathetic nervous system through breath-work, sound healing, chanting, and Yoga asanas that are gentle and slow. A yoga practice that can often involve lying down as you drift into a nurturing state of zenfulness. For Parkinson's, anything you can do to calm the sympathetic nervous system is key.

Aerial Yoga

Ever so daunting as we lay waiting in our Yoga Barn (Ubud, Bali) for our acrobatic instructor Pixie, to initiate a number of us newbies into the graceful, weightless form of aerial yoga. Having entered through the main pavilion made of traditional bamboo construction, I was relieved to see solid I-beam steel girders anchoring our six-metre high sling we were about to be suspended from. Imagine gently rotating upside down (without a harness) with the sling carefully positioned at the optimum balance point (somewhere between upper buttocks and hip). As you complete your inversion, remember which side of the sling to position your feet to lock yourself in (so that you don't go boom on your head). Now take one foot out while at the same time loop and cross your foot to the other side of the sling as you move into an inverted warrior pose. It was an awesome experience to accomplish!

Racquet Sports

There is emerging evidence of the importance of eye movement to activate the balance sensory system. *Racquet sports* such as Pickleball are a great way to maintain your hand-eye coordination. It is also a lower impact on your body than tennis and squash. If your legs are less mobile, table tennis is a great alternative. I am impressed to learn of the highly competitive *Ping Pong Parkinson*'s global community that comprises of 300 chapters (clubs) across 25 countries with an annual World Championships played out in differing host cities. See https://www.pingpongparkinson.org/

Immersion Therapy

As I learn how to breathe through a regulator strapped to scuba-diving equipment, I experience my first underwater *Immersion Therapy*. It was developed in 2017 by the South Australian based organisation *Determined2* see https://determined2.com.au/. Immersion Therapy is an innovative exercised-based therapy that expands on traditional hydrotherapy.

Gloop, gloop, the outside world becomes dull. Your focus becomes tunnel visioned while your mind calms as you become accustomed to the weightlessness and freedom. With increasing loss of fine-motor skills and upper body dexterity, finding multiple ways to exercise the neurological pathways while maintaining upper body strength is crucial for me. This therapy also happens to be high on the fun factor. A highlight was getting propelled along by the underwater *scooter*. Playing underwater darts with a foam torpedo as we ganged up against Marize, (our neurological physiotherapist who orchestrated this therapy) was also fun.

Something for amusement

Fascinated by the young hipsters in my local park walking a *slackline* suspended between two gum trees, I decided to give it a go. *Slacklining* combines balance and exercise with meditative qualities. In a park setting, the line (made of a 1 to 2 inch nylon webbing) is usually set just a few feet off the ground at the low mid point. But it is also a daredevil extreme sport with the use of *highlines* (often spanning across canyons). To be totally enthralled, see https://slackline.us/

Something for our brain

Oh, and don't forget to enjoy getting creative as you discover new ways to *exercise your mind*.

- After two years of formal classes studying Italian I now am reasonably self sufficient to enjoy my daily ritual of logging onto the Duolingo app. I continue to practise my Italian as I pitch myself against my online cohorts.

- Something I have recently started doing is holding a chess night at my home. Increasingly, I enjoy 1:1 catch-up time with friends. Chess nights combine my love of cooking for others followed by a mind challenging, combative game.

Have fun mixing it up as you develop your exercise regime. Actually, delete the word 'regime'. Don't become a slave to your exercise program. Be kind to yourself. Allow yourself to skip a day. Follow your energy levels and listen to your body. Keep pursuing your passions. Enjoy getting creative if you have to find a *work around*.

Just keep going. Try not to judge your changing ability.

Enjoy maintaining your balance in whatever way you can.

Nutrition

It would be totally understandable if your eyes glazed over as we all try to make sense of this medical explanation below:

> "Progressive dopaminergic neuronal cell loss in the substantia nigra pars compacta and widespread aggregation of the α-synuclein protein (encoded by the SNCA gene) in the form of Lewy bodies and Lewy neurites are the neuropathological hallmarks of Parkinson's disease".

Reading scientific journals can be so mind-numbingly overwhelming. So, let us push our thinking up a level and focus our attention on the following three key concepts that will help us come to grips with why nutrition is so important. These three concepts you may find useful as you consider options for your own symptom management:

- To understand **inflammatory** responses in the body and the flow-on effect.

- The importance of **gut health** and the well accepted linkage between the gut-brain axis.

- The concept of **mitophagy** and how a cell repairs or removes dysfunctional mitochondria and the potential to improve on the bodies repair process.

NUTRITION 67

Atkins, Pritikin, Mediterranean, Keto,
Think I'll go eat some worms.
Long ones, short ones, fat ones skinny ones,
Worms that squiggle and squirm.

Carnivore, Vego, Paleo, Vegan.
Wait a minute, I don't feel good,
I ate more worms than I probably should.

Gasp!

As we pick ourselves up and out of the quagmire, have you ever had that feeling of being slightly overwhelmed when it comes to diets?

Don't panic. You are most definitely not alone. And I am certainly not going to start by adding to the confusion. Rather, I would like to share with you some key principles that I follow.

Although there is some merit in many diets you'll come across including the ones shown in my poem above (although I am not so sure about the worms).
My first response to diets is that they are often all too hard for most of us to get our heads around and rarely do they empower us.
In fact, when I consider nutrition, I prefer not to even use the word 'diet'. Rather, I prefer to focus our understanding on what constitutes *good nutrition*? In doing so, I ask people to consider just one word.

With the knowledge that many chronic conditions are referred to as being an 'inflammatory disease', there is only one magic word to guide you, as and when you do your own extended reading on nutrition.

The magic word is *"Anti-inflammatory"*.

Anti-inflammatory Foods

So, now we can feel empowered to forget about diets per se but rather take the time to understand:

- Food groups that cause inflammation.

- Food groups that reduce inflammation.

- Consider portion size of certain food groups in relation to others on your dinner plate.

Once we understand these points, we can start to make informed decisions on what foods we consume.

Sometimes, it's not about removing a food group but knowing how to prepare and cook a food to make it more readily digestible.

Have you ever considered why there is a market for peeled tin tomatoes? Do you have Italian friends that roast their capsicums and discard the skins, or soak eggplant in brine? Many cultures will often twice cook chickpeas (a first boil to remove the skins).

Lentil eating cultures will soak and rinse their lentils often overnight and cook by using a pressure cooker. The Japanese are also known to soak and rinse their rice overnight. You might recall other food preparation techniques your grandmother use to do. I love it when I ask my foodie friends as to why they prepare things a certain way and the response comes back as "I don't know, we've always done it that way. Grandma always did it that way".

These traditional food preparation practices handed down through generations have all evolved for one express purpose. That purpose is to make our food more readily digestible.

Time to introduce the word 'lectins' as a key term. The above examples are all about trying to remove *lectins*. The goal is to minimise lectins while recognising it is nearly impossible to remove all lectins in your life. Lectins are a protein that your body cannot digest. You might know of people who don't like eating lentils as they experience bloating and gas. The gas is a result of the bodies inability to breakdown the lectins and leads to what is an inflammatory response. So, should we eat lentils? Absolutely, they are wonderfully nutritious. Replaying my earlier comment on preparation. I will always soak my lentils overnight to significantly reduce lectins. Also by using a pressure cooker with the high concentration of heat will remove pretty much any remnants of lectins. Consider this as you tour through remote villages of lentil eating nations and observe how they cook.

Pressure cookers are highly efficient. I generally cook in bulk and freeze into meal sized portions to use as a base. This allows me to defrost a portion into a saucepan to have a ready-made meal in 10 minutes. I augment my base lentil soups with a favourite protein of usually chicken or fish. My hack on fish, is to dice the fresh fish and place the raw pieces directly into a bowl and ladle in the piping hot lentil soup. By the time the soup is at eating temperature (3 to 5 minutes) the fish will be beautifully cooked. Sometimes, I will add fresh greens such as broccoli, kale, silverbeat, or amaranth. I will often make a pulled pork version. Yum, totally nourishing!

Understanding Sugar and Inflammation

Often when I ask others as to how much sugar they have most will recount how much raw sugar they physically add, with comments like "Oh, I don't have much. I just have one sugar in my coffee".

Sugar is right up there as one of the most inflammatory foods you can consume. So, without wanting to come across as a kill-joy, for the sake of your health, it is worthwhile that we delve into sugar a little further.

What other forms of sugars are there?

Before I knew what I know now, I'll provide the following story. I happened to cook up a large serving of my home made penne ragu for a musician friend who had come for lunch. My friend happens to be diabetic. The lunch whilst well received sent my friend into an insulin spike. So, what actually happened? After all, I hadn't cooked with added sugar.

I soon got to learn that the body will break down carbohydrates and convert them into glucose and that glucose is of course sugar. So, our carbohydrate laden lunch with the mountainous serving of penne pasta was the culprit. Therefore, this is also where the thinking around *portion size* comes in to play.

What does your dinner plate look like?

When you have a stir-fry does your plate have 80% rice with 20% vegetables. My plate will be 10% rice and 90% vegetables. And while we are talking about rice (and other forms of carbohydrates) let's discuss the importance of the *glycemic index (GI)*.

GI is a ranking system for carbohydrates to indicate how readily they affect blood sugar levels.

A goal, where practical, is to choose carbohydrates that have a lower GI. Carbohydrates with a lower GI are absorbed more slowly resulting in a slower rise in blood sugar levels. By example, if you enjoy white rice, try using basmati rice that has a lower GI. You could swap out potatoes for sweet potatoes. Have fun learning about low GI carbohydrates and in creating healthier options. And think about portion size and your ratio of carbohydrates to protein.

Fructose is Sugar

Caveman didn't roll out of his skin slung bed and help himself to a mammoth sized orange juice (3 to 6 oranges) every morning. This is a guaranteed way to give yourself an insulin spike, to raise your blood sugar levels, and contribute to inflammation in the body. The trick is to be mindful of how much fruit you consume and when. I mainly consume fruits that provide the best trade-off between fructose and nutrients. My morning breakfast of seeds and ancient grains will mainly be topped with blueberries (and coconut yoghurt). Bananas are a wonderfully rich food source. Unless you are swinging through the trees every day, be mindful of when and how much you consume. I tend to only have bananas on a sport day when my body will make use of the energy.

Consider not having apples, pears, oranges, melons and grapes with your main meal (or straight after). Again, this just adds to an insulin spike and disrupts how your body will store and prioritise nutrient take-up. The best time to consume fruits is when your body has a natural slump in energy levels. That is, late morning and late afternoon (and well outside of main meal times). I will often have one medjool date at these times. (A cautionary note on medjool dates. Go easy on them. They are a powerhouse of goodness. Although they are lower in GI, one at a time is enough unless you are about to do a marathon).

So, have you been a sugar fein all your life? Please don't make yourself miserable. Just set your own realistic goals to incrementally reduce sugar out of your life. Every improvement is a positive step in the right direction.

Gut Health and the Gut-Brain Axis

Regardless of whether you have a chronic illness, gut health (gut microbiome) is such an important area of health for everyone.

The medical profession universally agree on the linkage between the gut and brain axis.

I won't go into more detail here as I have dedicated chapter 7 (titled, G.I.N.) that specifically looks into the syndicated research efforts between gastroenterology, immunology, and neurology and why this is so important.

What is most relevant at this point is to consider nutrition from a gut microbiome perspective. To ensure that you introduce as much biodiversity through your foods as possible.

Mitophagy, a Compromised Process in PD

A segway into mitophagy is to touch on *mitochondria* first.

So, what is *mitochondria* and why is it so important?

Mitochondria is often referred to as the "powerhouse of cells". They produce energy in the form of *adenosine triphosphate* (ATP).

"Mitochondrial dysfunction is a core hallmark of PD (Parkinson's disease)".

I will leave links to scientific articles. However, my intent here is to encourage others to further your knowledge on mitochondria and to understand how nutrition can better support *mitochondria health* and reduce *oxidative stress.*

An important caveat is that *I am not suggesting for a moment that nutrition is a cure for a chronic illness.* Nevertheless, whatever we can do to foster improved mitochondrial function is all positive.

As you further your understanding on mitochondria you will understand why some people espouse taking cold showers, ice baths, and practice intermittent fasting.

Mitophagy is the process of removing damaged mitochondria. This process is thought to be compromised in Parkinson's disease. The result is a build up of malformed proteins that progressively damage and cause the death of dopaminergic neurons. We all need dopaminergic neurons to allow our bodies to move and control bodily functions.

For those with a thirst for the scientific detail, I provide the following journals.

Henrich et al. "Mitochondrial dysfunction in Parkinson's disease – a key disease hallmark with therapeutic potential". *Molecular Neurodegeneration*, 18:83, (2023).

Liu et al, "Mitophagy in Parkinson's Disease: From Pathogenesis to Treatment". In *Cells.* 2019 Jul 12;8(7):712.

Often just reading the 'abstract' and 'conclusion' is enough to get the salient points.

Nutrition is such a broad and evolving topic on one hand. On the other, if we go back to basics, we find nothing has ever changed when it comes down to good nutrition. What is known is that caveman received infinitely more biodiversity from their food sources than what we do today.

Hence, my preoccupation in applying *harmony in motion* in everyday life – *empowering* myself and others, *positively questioning*, while seeking *restorative* solutions.

What I have tried to establish in this chapter is a point of focus, to leave enough of a trail of breadcrumbs that are easy to consume and follow up on as you do your own extended reading on the topic of nutrition. While at the same time, being conscious that the core premise behind this book is one of *empowerment*.

Wishing you much health as you explore your evolving nutrition.

Keep this one word in the forefront, 'anti-inflammatory'.

Nourish Yourself. Your Mitochondria will Thank You!

Mindfulness

MINDFULNESS

Crosslegged upon my yoga cushion within a calm, safe, sacred spot in front of my midcentury low Chinese Elm scroll table, I mindfully pour from black cast iron my morning ginger and cardamon tea.

Gazing at a collection of seashells and the intricate detail of potted green. Presenting a visual reminder of the natural order and harmony in nature, and with much to feel blessed and thankful for.

Mindfulness for me is very much about being truly present, practicing gratitude, and being attuned to your every waking thought. It is also about maintaining a zen state of mind, easing the body into the morning glow, absent of stimuli. No coffee, music, and scrolling tech for my first hour and a half in favour of stillness.

Hydrate, breathe, meditate, and nourish yourself. My morning ritual is quiet and nurturing to both body and soul.

It is interesting how calm my symptoms remain while in this state of bliss.

Thoughts of "Oh no, is that the time. I am now late for my exercise class" is likely to raise cortisol levels. As I race to pick up my phone [Scroll, scroll, Click... scroll, scroll, Click...]. I catch myself from falling as I slump into my chair. My right-hand tremor starts to become pronounced. My right leg is in unison with my left thumb twitching.

So, what exactly happened to create such a change from calm?

Our thoughts!

Thoughts that created a sense of panic or urgency which in turn translates to a spike in cortisol.

Produced by the adrenal glands, cortisol is a hormone that plays a crucial role in metabolism, immune response, and stress regulation. Cortisol is part of our normal daily rhythm that peaks in the morning to help us wake up, and ideally tapers off during the day. What we need to be mindful of is to avoid unnecessary cortisol spikes and avoid maintaining high-levels.

In Parkinson's there really is no such thing as good elevated levels of cortisol. An enthusiastic drive in my manual sports car while running late for my physiotherapist will give me a cortisol spike that will exacerbate my symptoms. Racing a go-kart is high on fun-factor, but will translate to increased cortisol and symptoms. I am definitely not saying to just curl up with your feline on a couch. It is more about understanding your body, calming your thoughts, and exercising and engaging in fun activities in a manner that minimises elevated cortisol levels.

What safety nets can we put in place so as not to feel rushed? Is anything in your life really that important? Most things on a daily basis are often not time sensitive. Look for ways to alleviate time pressures in your life. As a positive reinforcement I practice these words, *"Forget about everything, nothing really matters"*.

More on my favourite racquet sport later, but worthwhile to

note that I am able to compete in tournaments in a manner that doesn't significantly create a cortisol spike. I achieve this primarily through focusing on mindset. Staying objective about the game, maintaining a state of calm, playing in a very zen-like state, and between games I will practice diaphragmatic breathing and meditate.

> As we become more aware of our thoughts, we can learn to influence our cortisol levels.

Mindfulness is very much about being aware of our thoughts and emotions. How we respond. Do we in fact respond at all? Or, do we become the quiet observer sitting with our thoughts and allowing our emotions to be fully expressed. We don't have to solve everything. Not every thought requires an answer. Acknowledgement and self reflection without judgement are more important.

Let's pause for a moment and consider the two branches of the Autonomic Nervous System, the *sympathetic* versus *parasympathetic,* and the relationship between them. Can mindfulness play a role?

To illustrate the sympathetic nervous system in action, I'm reminded of a six-day hike through our First Nation people's

Jawoyn country in the Northern Territory on a remote trail called Jatbula (just north of Katherine). As we assembled at the park ranger's office, we casually asked if there where any predators out there we should be aware of. We were reassured that on day 1, once we reached the sandstone plateau above Biddlecombe Cascades, we would no longer need to worry about the freshwater crocodiles.

In tune, we all said, "Anything else?"

"Oh well, there are wild boar you need to keep your distance from."

"So, what do we do if we see one?"

"I suggest you run and find the nearest tree!"

"And how would we know if they are around?"

"If you see fresh dung, you know they are very close, probably within 50-100 metres."

On day 5, somewhere between Sandy Camp and Sweetwater Pool, conversations were jovial as we ambled along until it happened. We all stopped dead in our tracks at once. Steaming in front of us in the searing sun was the biggest and most fresh pile of dung. With eyes darting, we scoured our surrounds. We needed no reminder of the plan to run for the nearest tree. There was only one problem with this plan.

We were now in the middle of a vast and open grass savanna with a smattering of pencil thin trees no taller than 3 or 4 metres. I had visions of 6 hikers up one of these spindly looking trees complete with packs on. The tree bowing perilously towards the ground with a wild boar looking up at us (like *Alice in Wonderland's* Cheshire Cat) with a mischievous grin licking his chops.

Panic subsided when I realised that I didn't have to outrun the boar. I just had to out run my mates, LOL. :-)

So, back to our sympathetic nervous system and let us examine what actually happened. Our bodies went into *fight or flight* mode. Our heart rate spiked in unison as our pulse rate climbed, hair bristled, our adrenal glands worked overtime, our pupils dilated, non essential body functions shut down, and with increased blood flow to vital organs our minds were now racing in a heightened state of alert.

In contrast, our *parasympathetic nervous* system, is there to counter and help reduce stress. Once we came to the realisation that there was no pending doom and gloom (no immediate threat from said wild boar), it was time for some deep diaphragmatic breathing to start the process of calming our elevated sympathetic nervous system. Once at our Sweet Water Pool campsite, the pristine environment was very conducive for deep relaxation and literal grounding as we walked with naked abandonment beneath the trees to recline in one of the endless crystal clear pools. With a listful gaze through dappled sunlight, it was time to meditate.

I was safe. Through self awareness and applying these nurturing techniques, we had now activated the parasympathetic nervous system as we invoked a deeper sense of calm and tranquility.

Mindfulness might have kept us a little more objective. The boar was probably more scared of us. None of us actually ever saw the wild boar. We had collectively allowed our thoughts and belief systems to throw us into panic.

Pause, breathe, take stock. Don't allow the wild boars in your life get a hold of you.

Chapter 7
G.I.N.

Immerse Yourself in Knowledge

As a young lad, I recall looking down the lens of my father's microscope (a *Beck London Model 47 Made in England*) in his surgery. It was an era when your local GP did basic pathology. Badgering Dad, we submitted our finger for a skin prick so that we could smear a drop on a Belgium-made glass micro-slide and view our blood. I used to love sneaking into Dad's surgery (that adjoined our home) to have a chat with the 'live' full size skeleton (OK, it was alive to me and it was indeed the bones of a once living person).

Dad was always fun and wonderfully caring as a GP. When he used the otoscope on us kids, he would get us to hold up two fingers in front of one ear while he looked through the other. It was always followed by his reassuring words "Yep, it is all clear. I can see two fingers." ;-)

Being raised in a medical family gave me some perspective on matters of health.

I can still hear the wise words of my mother "Prevention is better than cure", who trained as a nurse prior to penicillin and the much innovation we have today in patient care.

As a technologist, I hold a deep fascination at the rate of change and how technology is allowing the human race to solve complex problems. For the medical scientific research community, we are witnessing computational tools to collect and analyse volumes of data at a scale previously not achieved.

The collection of data is no longer a technical impediment. Establishing the right protocol (preferably at the point of diagnosis and prior) to collect baseline data becomes critical (through coordinated efforts) to better understand Parkinson's and the progression.

Diagnosed with Parkinson's in 2018 was the catalyst for me to educate myself of this degenerative condition that currently has no cure or disease modifying therapies. To positively question, make informed decisions, and focus my energy on what I can do to bring about greater awareness of this chronic illness.

> *"All disease begins in the gut"*
> *~ Hippocrates (c. 460-370 BC)*

Prior to my diagnosis I had been aware of the ground breaking work by Monash University in creating the *FODMAP* and Monash's global position in understanding nutrition and gut microbiome.

A quick reminder on FODMAP (Source: https://www.monashfodmap.com/):

- *FODMAP stands for Fermentable Oligosaccharides, Disaccharides, Monosaccharides, and Polyols.*
  It refers to a group of short-chain carbohydrates that are

poorly absorbed in the small intestine and can cause digestive issues like bloating, gas, and diarrhea, especially in people with IBS (irritable bowel syndrome).

The ancient Greek physician Hippocrates (acknowledged for his foundational teachings for modern medicine) made the claim over 2,000 years ago that "*All disease begins in the gut.*"

Early in my diagnosis, I had the good fortune to be introduced to the Monash Bio Medical Sciences labs including the work Monash were doing in relation to Parkinson's and the whole gut-immune-brain axis. I received wonderful insights into what is thought to be biologically occurring in Parkinson's and therefore, the key research directions.

When you start to immerse yourself in the pursuit of knowledge with genuine curiosity and enthusiasm, it is interesting the things that happen as you surround yourself with like-minded people. I take the approach of thinking through how I can contribute as well.

When I spoke earlier about mindfulness, I referred to the idea of "Observing and maintaining a complete separation of your mind to that of your body". When I meet with clinicians, medical research doctors, students (the next generation of clinicians), data scientists, and the scientific community, conversations become more collaborative, part of the same team. We share experiences to solve what's happening to my body.

Through my involvement with Monash, I got to meet the aspiring executive team and department heads of the newly formed

GIN Discovery Program that formally brings together *Gastroenterology | Immunology | Neuroscience*. With their mission to:

> *Combat Complex Health Conditions Through Cutting-Edge Research of the Gut-Immune-Brain Axis*
> *~ GIN Discovery Program, Monash University*

It is universally agreed that there is a correlation between *the gut and brain axis* for neurological conditions such as Alzheimer's, multiple sclerosis, Parkinson's, and many other chronic conditions.

Melbourne has been acknowledged as a global epicentre for medical research. I have personally witnessed the collaboration between Monash University, The Florey Institute of Neuroscience and Mental Health, Melbourne University, WEHI (Walter & Eliza Hall Institute of Medical Research), Deakin University, and the Baker Heart & Diabetes Institute.

Yes, a diabetes institute! I became aware that Type 1 diabetes is an autoimmune condition attacking the insulin producing beta cells in the pancreas leading to little or no insulin production.

At a Monash symposium, I got to meet the auspices at Deakin University behind the *Food & Mood Centre* program (https://foodandmoodcentre.com.au). The program provides an extensive multidisciplinary research approach that has scientifically established the link between gut-microbiome for anxiety and depression. They have been able to show how diet can greatly improve symptom management.

Dysbiosis refers to an imbalance in gut bacteria (microbiome). Such an imbalance is said to influence neuroinflammation and neurotransmitter production impacting on overall brain function. You'll now understand my preoccupation with following an *anti-inflammatory* focus on the foods I choose to eat.

A Positive Outlook

- The gut-immune-brain axis is understood which creates the opportunity for much continued, focused research.

- There is an opportunity to create a paradigm shift in the protocol at diagnosis to capture meaningful baseline data.

- To adequately capture the anecdotal evidence and translate to measured scientific based outcomes.

- We can now measure biomarkers with a high degree of accuracy for Parkinson's disease. This creates the opportunity to accelerate our understanding in disease prevention and/or delay the onset.

As the medical science and research community moves increasingly towards a *foundation* based funding model (philanthropy and grants versus a pure commercial model), society benefits by removing barriers that fosters greater collaboration for rapid innovation. This approach greatly enhances the probability for a cure and more precision based (tailored) treatments.

According to a study published in The BMJ, researchers from Capital Medical University in Beijing projected that the global prevalence of Parkinson's disease will reach 25.2 million cases by 2050, marking a 112% increase from 2021, (see su et al, *"Projections for prevalence of Parkinson's disease and its driving factors in 195 countries and territories to 2050: modelling study of Global Burden of Disease Study 2021" in British Medical Journal.* BMJ 2025;388:e080952).

Awareness and understanding of the need for accelerated focus and attention for Parkinson's research and funding is gaining momentum.

- *The global collaborative research initiative for Parkinson's disease is known as Aligning Science Across Parkinson's (ASAP). Launched in 2019, ASAP aims to accelerate the pace of discovery and inform the path to a cure through fostering collaboration, generating research-enabling resources, and promoting data sharing among the scientific community.*

    A key component of ASAP is the Collaborative Research Network (CRN). An international, multidisciplinary network of research teams addressing high-priority research questions to advance the understanding of Parkinson's

> disease and drive new ideas into the research and development pipeline.

> - In June 2024, The Australian Federal Government has announced funding to develop and implement Australia's first National Parkinson's action plan.

Significant milestones are being made that is guiding the research directions in unraveling Parkinson's disease, onset and progression.

> - In 2023, the Michael J. Fox Foundation for Parkinson's Research (MJFF) announced a significant breakthrough in the quest for a Parkinson's disease biomarker. Researchers developed the alpha-synuclein seed amplification assay (αSyn-SAA), a test that detects the presence of abnormal alpha-synuclein proteins—a hallmark of Parkinson's disease—in cerebrospinal fluid. This advancement enables earlier and more accurate diagnosis, even before clinical symptoms manifest, potentially transforming patient care and accelerating the development of new therapies.
> [Reference: Michael J. Fox Foundation @michaeljfoxfoundation.org "...Parkinson's Disease Biomarker Found" published 13th April 2023. https://www.michaeljfox.org/news/breaking-news-parkinsons-disease-biomarker-found]

> - March 2025, Researchers at the Walter and Eliza Hall Institute (WEHI) have achieved a significant milestone in Parkinson's disease research by determining the structure of the human PINK1 protein and understanding how it

activates upon binding to damaged mitochondria. This discovery offers new avenues for developing treatments aimed at slowing or halting the progression of Parkinson's disease.

PINK1 plays a crucial role in identifying and marking damaged mitochondria for removal—a process essential for cellular health. Mutations in the PINK1 gene can disrupt this function, leading to the accumulation of defective mitochondria, which is associated with the onset of Parkinson's disease.

By visualising the structure of PINK1 and elucidating its activation mechanism, the WEHI team has provided valuable insights into the molecular underpinnings of Parkinson's. This foundational knowledge paves the way for the development of targeted therapies that could enhance PINK1 function or correct its deficiencies, offering hope for more effective treatments in the future.
[Reference: WEHI "Scientists solve decades-long Parkinson's mystery" published 14th March 2025 https://www.wehi.edu.au/news/scientists-solve-decades-long-parkinsons-mystery/]

With all this wonderful collaboration and opportunity of significant medical advancements in the treatment (and potential cure) for many chronic conditions, I offer this very gentle reminder on mindfulness:

- *I find it crucial to not obsess unduly as to whether there will be a cure for Parkinson's within my lifetime. It is enough for me to know that there is much syndicated efforts all pulling together in the right direction. I will continue to create opportunities for myself to be involved and provide input.*

- *It is so important to remain truly present and practice gratitude for what we can do today.*

- *Feel empowered in defining and creating our own meaningful life.*

I deliver these words with absolute care and compassion from a position of deep and personal understanding.

Enjoy immersing yourself in knowledge!

Chapter 8
Inspiring Others to Live in Natural Harmony

I love hearing stories of grandparents who missed the computerisation era in their workplace environment to see them make the step change in becoming highly proficient. For example, with an iPad they connect with loved ones on FaceTime or download an app to watch the World Cup. The adoption cycle of technology for all of us comes down to timing, relevancy, and purpose. I was relatively late to Instagram. However, in November 2022, I had a growing sense of an intended purpose.

I trade marked the name *NATRAOMI* ®. I loosely based this made-up word from the Italian *armonia naturale* which translates to *natural harmony. (The deeper thinking behind the subtitle of this book will now become apparent)*. #NATRAOMI was created partly for cathartic reasons and a form of journaling as I navigate through my own Parkinson's, I ultimately was looking for a non invasive way to share my story. I like the way Instagram allows me to set up an account where users can look at my posts anonymously without necessarily having to follow.

With the intent to help others in need, I set out to foster a broader community of care and wellbeing. I wanted to encourage and inspire others to grab back a degree of control over their own chronic condition.

I have captured the following words in my tagline that really resonated for me along my journey. Specifically, words of affirmation that instil a message of *positivity* which I would dearly love others to fully internalise and own for themselves as you boldly step forward.

EMPOWERING | POSITIVELY QUESTIONING | RESTORATIVE

The logo for *NATRAOMI* ® is an *Aloe polyphylla*. I chose to use a five pointed stylised interpretation. This cactus has a stunningly symmetrical spiral growth habit. So, why did I choose to use five points in my logo design? Why is the number five so important? Five happens to be part of the Fibonacci sequence. Stay with me for a bit and I'll explain. Each number in the Fibonacci sequence is derived by adding the two proceeding numbers. Starting at zero, the sequence becomes 0, 1, 1, 2, 3, 5, 8, 13, 21, 34... You are correct if you deduced that the next number is 55 and that the sequence logically continues on into infinity.

So, where do we see the Fibonacci sequence come into play?

When we consider nature and the concept of randomness it is interesting to question just how random things are. Is there in fact a blue print, a natural sequence and harmony in all living organisms and matter?

For example, I encourage you to have fun counting the spirals of a sunflower and you will find that the display of its florets are in perfect spirals of 55, 34, and 21, which follow the Fibonacci sequence precisely. Now, grab a pine cone or a pineapple, and as you count the fruitlets, you'll see they end in a Fibonacci sequence.

As we stand in awe watching the courageous surfers chase the tube waves to be engulfed into another dimension, know that the curvature of all waves can be mathematically mapped to the

96 BALANCE IN MOTION

Fibonacci sequence. Perhaps even more astonishingly, so can the galaxy above us. This spiral effect is related to the golden ratio (or golden mean) that is often adopted by architects, artists, and photographers to create visually pleasing work based on balance and symmetry.

When you study the intricate segments that can be seen when you dissect a nautilus shell, what will you see? As the nautilus shell continues to grow, with each succeeding spiral segment another Fibonacci sequence is added.

The renaissance artist and scientist Leonardo da Vinci's (c. 1490) depiction of the *Vitruvian Man* (superimposed in two positions and overlayed in a circle and a square) was created to illustrate the symmetry and proportions of the human form. Leonardo's drawing is based upon the writings of the ancient 1st century Roman architect and engineer *Vitruvius*. Vitruvius is well regarded as producing the first book on architectural theory through his multi-volume work titled *De Architectura* where he discusses the notion of perfect proportions[1].

The closer we get to not meddling with nature, the more we move closer to natural harmony in all aspects of our lives.

---

1. If you take a ruler to the print version of this book you will see that it is precisely 5 inches by 8 inches. Both 5 and 8 are part of the Fibonacci sequence and not surprising that this ratio is known to be aesthetically pleasing to the human eye.

Chapter 9
Finding Your Happiness

B eyond the canvas of Monèt's Water Lilies, I observe my life.

The importance of community (whilst always with me) became paramount post diagnosis as I set out to accelerate my involvement in both **building and participating in community**.

To be human, to create a balanced life, is the desire to want to **connect** with one another. I intentionally emphasis the word 'connect'. The mid-century American psychologist Abraham Maslow portrayed in his *Hierarchy of Needs*, that after our base needs are met (food, water, shelter), the next layer of psychological need is a sense of belonging (love and connection).
A smile from a stranger on a tram is one form of connection that maybe as valid as a life-long childhood friendship. When a stranger comes to your aide as your bag gets jammed in the tram door because your shuffle didn't allow for a quick enough exit, is that person really a stranger? Could it be that person had tremendous empathy for you for reasons not apparent? We are all connected in this world somehow.

The Water Lilies are a metaphor for my sense of community.

As I wistfully gaze at a lily pad I see my motorcycle group. Another lily pad represents my hike group. Another my jazz friends, the community garden group, dance friends, mountain biking, my car club (of whom many I have club raced with since the eighties), to new blossoming lily pads like my Pickleball community and Italian group.

The tranquility of my pond, my community, my solace...

On occasion, the caressing breeze generates enough ripple effect for some lily pads to intersect and cross pollinate.

All in a Day

Tea ceremony, meditation, nourishing breakfast parfait, I cherish my morning ritual.

Thinking fond memories of my father who had passed away on this day five years earlier (three months after his 90th birthday). Dad was a remarkable man (retiring to Darwin from Melbourne in the latter 24 years of his life). He understood the importance of exercise and the power of community.

For his final weeks curtain call, he had played his weekly game of Sunday tennis with mates and participated in two choir rehearsals.

In front of the chair which dad had donated to the Darwin Bicentennial Gardens (in a spot that is rather aptly named 'Doctors Gully'), I invited guests to take turns in spreading out the letters R-E-G in the lawn with dad's ashes. As my brother and I walked back to dad's apartment (with grey plastic container in hand that had moments earlier contained dad's ashes), we both looked at each other with the same twinkle in our eyes and a wondrous sense of mischievousness that we had inherited from dad. Without a word spoken, we lifted the yellow lid of the recycle bin and tipped our hats to dad as we bid farewell to the canister. We intuitively knew dad would have approved. Dad loved living light. He also cared very much about the impact humans have on this planet and how much space and time we should reasonably take up.

I digress, now back to today. I was excited to know I had a wonderful evening engagement party to attend.

Would panic set in when you knew you had to buy a card and a gift at the last minute?

No need to panic, take joy in the process. Think of the source of friendship and inspiration will come.
I knew that it was market day at my local Community Environment Park called CERES (for more about CERES, see chapter 13 *The Plot Thickens*).
Perfect! To be immersed in the beautiful community gardens and cafe, to the backdrop of gorgeous young musicians, created the opportunity to wander up and connect with stall holders and purchase a hand crafted card from Jana (who was very kind in reminding me that she followed me on Instagram as her aunt has Parkinson's).

My favourite ceramicist was not there, so plan B on gift.

Living in inner Melbourne I am spoilt for choice with seven organic shops within a 2-kilometre radius. It was time for a nourishing cocoa and berry smoothie with coconut milk at another one of my favourite organic shops in my neighbouring suburb. I knew I'd be able to find a gift in the homeware shop adjacent.

A common story. As I sat down to my smoothie, a lady in her 70s who had arrived on two sticks kindly asked if I was OK, having observed my difficulty in walking to the communal bench (with my smoothie becoming more like a thick-shake).

I thanked her for asking, reassured her I was OK, and that I just had Parkinson's.
"Do you have a moment to talk?", came the reply, "I think I have Parkinson's". After taking the time to listen to 'D', it became evident that she did in fact know that she had Parkinson's and was taking one of the main compounding drugs of levodopa for the past three years. "I haven't told anyone, I don't want to be a burden to people, I don't want others to view me differently", D went on to say. After some kind words, I reminded her that none of us need to live our lives by the 'shoulds'. We don't act on things or tell people things because we think we should. She smiled, thanked me, and asked for my number. Isolation within our communities is real (regardless of health conditions). When we take the time to slow down from our often too hectic lives, we start to observe the environment before us with more insight and connect more deeply with those around us.

> ***When we live by our authentic self and walk this planet with an open heart centre, we will find much happiness and contentment.***
> ***Don't be surprised when you find that others are drawn to you.***

My neighbour popped in briefly to help me re-pot some fledgling plants. OK, I confess to killing a succulent plant – actually six succulents which is quite the achievement. ;-/
Take pleasure in the smallest of things. See the beauty in everything. Surround yourself in greenery.

The evening engagement party was an awesome occasion connecting with so many old dance friends from 10, 15, and 20 years ago. It was a heartwarming reminder of the importance of long-term friendships and maintaining connections. My gift card read, *"This small gift is a symbol of how well you fit together. Hand-forged as a reminder of how unique you both are and the combined creative talent you share"*.
You don't need ChatGPT when you focus on the source of your friendship, and be your authentic self.

Home by 9:00pm. Half an hour to recalibrate, followed by a solid two hours of writing.

A seemingly packed day, but was is it really?

So, why was I not exhausted?

Life's Learnings

- When we follow our heart, we experience natural harmony and flow to our day.

- As we slow down to interact with our environment, we see the beauty in everything and allow ourselves to be truly present in our interactions.

- If we stay objective and maintain a balanced view (don't judge, but rather seek to understand), while being kind and curious to everyone, we are no longer in conflict with the world around us.

- Once we realise that we are only on this planet to give and receive love, walk lightly with an open heart, and a state of happiness will flow in abundance as you give and receive love.

- When we are being our authentic self and are attuned to our own priorities in life, we will find contentment. We will become more receptive to observe and practice gratitude.

You might like to have fun taking these life learnings as you reflect on your day (or perhaps as you re-read the account of my day).

I very much related to the 2023 film, *Perfect Days*, directed by the Wim Wenders (who is regarded as part of the New German Cinema movement of the 1970s and is known for his deeply contemplative films).

Perfect Days is a wonderfully gentle film exploring an exemplary notion of happiness.

The synopsis reads:
"Hirayama [the central character], feels content with his life as a toilet cleaner in Tokyo. Outside of his structured routine, he cherishes music on cassette tapes, reads books and takes photos. Through unexpected encounters, he reflects on finding beauty in the world".

Wishing you many Hirayama moments in your day.

Chapter 10
Wellness

In a letter to his son Eduard on the 5th February 1930, Albert Einstein stated, *"Life is like riding a bicycle. To keep your balance, you must keep moving"*.

Beyond the literal interpretation, it is argued that it was rather sage advice from a father to a son, to embrace life's journey with optimism and self determination, to stay present and practice gratitude while maintaining a positive mindset.

Wellness is about maintaining a sense of equilibrium, maintaining a balanced outlook with a healthy perspective and objectivity.

A decade ago for my 50th, I decided upon a Sanskrit OM symbol tattoo on my left forearm as I pursued a deeper connection with ancient wisdom and my own spirituality. In Hinduism and Buddhism, the OM is a sacred sound representing the vibration of life and the interconnectedness of all states of consciousness and the universe. As you explore your conscious, subconscious, and unconscious states of mind (represented by the three curves of the OM symbol), the semi-circle represents *Maya*, the illusion we create which separates the individual self from the ultimate reality. The shape at the top of the symbol represents *Turiya*, a fourth state of consciousness derived by a state of bliss and attainment of ultimate reality.

By 2024, I felt that I had accomplished a lot with my understanding of nutrition (while recognising that nutrition is a constant refinement as we remain attuned to our bodies).

I am blessed to have had an active life through my varied interests. Exercise has been a continuum, albeit with some adjustments over recent years as I embrace change while my body increasingly misbehaves.

Under the guise of Wellness, the key pillar that I wanted to set my intentions around (to further my skill and deepen my practice on) was *mindfulness*.

With a wonderful start to the new year staying with dear friends in Harrietville, who created warmth beyond the atmospherics of their cosy mud-brick home. Supported by Greg, we did a seven kilometre day hike (ramble), along the stunningly beautiful Razor Back trail that leads to Mount Feathertop.

Is it important that I may never be able to carry the weight of an overnight pack once more and camp out under my own steam. Here I was in absolute paradise, atop of one of my most favourite vantage points in the Australian alps, soaring high with the wedge-tailed eagles.

As I retrospectively posted my Instagram reel, the soulful words from musician and composer Holly Kluge (Rochester, NY) of her 2012 recording of *Happy Little Things* fitted beautifully, capturing the very essence of my experience. As I stood upon the alpine ridge of high, I drank in the fresh embracing air and endless vista, surrounded by a sea of yellow daisies. I laid back basking in the sun while munching on my homemade nourishing snack pack. At the same time I vacantly looked towards the blue sky caressed by cotton wool clouds. I was transported back to childhood memories of endless carefree moments lying on our backyard trampoline gazing skywards, creating images out of the fluffy clouds.

The inspiring words of Holly's tune are a beautiful reminder and are worthwhile replaying here:

Don't forget the little things in life that make you happy
Don't forget the little things in life that make you smile
Oh, cast your cares aside and think about the things that make you smile
Big white puffy clouds in a big blue sky,
Findin' as many cloud pictures as you can find
Happy yellow flowers and a homemade pie
Oh, don't forget the happy little things

"Happy Little Things" ~ Holly Kluge, 2012

Rekindling your child like fascination for the world around you is such a beautiful way to bring balance and joy as you channel your thoughts to where you are now. To be truely present and thankful for the experiences you can have today. To fully embrace change and focus on what you can do rather than magnifying what you can no longer do.

A midst ancient tall timbers, with naked abandonment I descend within. Transformative, reflective, restorative, as I gently touch the earth of the Labyrinth's circular stone path. With each successive step, taking the time to pause until my tremor calms. An opportunity to completely let go, allowing all thoughts of naked self-consciousness to dissolve, deferring rather to a deep transcending meditative state, blissfully immersed in natures beauty.

It was a totally sensual and grounding experience to have spent time at the Yarra Valley Living Centre (YVLC). The centre was established by the remarkable (cancer survivor) Dr Ian Gawler in the 1970s. Since 2021, the YVLC continues under the guidance of the international organisation Brahma Kumaris offering beyond meditation a variety of wellness programs, retreats, and courses.

By mid year, I had set my sights on travelling to a place of spirituality where I could experience a concentration of differing wellness modalities, as part of my overall approach to self-care and continual journey of spiritual enlightenment.

Reclined in my Bali, safe and secure in a sanctuary fortified of rice fields proud. The gentle ripples of the plunge pool begin to twinkle as the long early rays filter through scattered palms afar. As the blades of green become translucent in the morning glow I step lightly along the foot wide paddy walls to take up my now sacred place for sun salutations. Giving thanks and gratitude for all that I am and how blessed I feel to be here.

Breathtaking, the reward of meandering through a canopy of green, up the vertical climb of precisely 55-stone steps (seemingly laid in random), from the rice field canal to my private rice paddy villa. Located in the peaceful farming community of Tegallalang, just 15 minutes outside of Ubud, in Bali. The region of Ubud is set inland surrounded by lush vegetation and dense forests. The fertile soils of chocolate brown provides the ideal environment for agriculture, and hence the predominance of rice terraces. Notably, the region has historical significance for the Balinese for its spirituality, and energy healing, with an abundance of herbs and plants offering medicinal properties. Ubud is derived by the Balinese word Ubad, which means *medicine*.

Purposefully staying in close proximity to the wonderful *Pyramids of Chi*, where I spent much of my time. Created by visionaries Peter and Lynn, who held a deep fascination for the power and energy of pyramids and inspired by ancient sound healing, when they conceived the idea for this world-class sound healing and wellness heaven. Your experience (like mine) will undoubtable live up to their tagline "Expect the Unexpected".

> "Give unconditionally, receive divinely"
> ~ Maitreya Prema

The grandeur of the triangular panels rising to an apex created a sense of infinity within our pyramid. Upon our meditation cushions, we sat in a semi-circle allowing for intimacy and connection. Our small group developed a rare bond of care and contemplation facilitated by the generosity and authenticity of Maitreya. We were here to experience the ancient Indian restorative practice of *seven chakras*. It is said, that each of the seven chakras represent energy centres within our bodies that govern a specific physical, emotional, and spiritual aspect of our being.

We were lying on a yoga mat for the concluding phase of our practice. It was not sleep inducing, but rather with full awareness as I drifted into such a zen like state, surpassing any previous level I had ever experienced. As our session closed, I became aware that I needed to maintain quiet. I opted to wander through the gardens and delay my nourishing lunch, the salivating soul-food provided at the Pyramids Cafe.

Maitreya was born in India and raised in a spiritual family, initiated at a very young age by enlightened masters, he spent many years in ashrams to support meditations and healing journeys. Later, he wandered in the Himalayas, learning how to serve from the heart and he returned carrying a gift that is able to shift people *from overthinking of the mind* to the calmness of the mind.

This latter point of calming the 'overthinking mind' whilst relevant to all of us becomes intrinsic for those of us with Parkinson's, in seeking a myriad of ways to calm the sympathetic nervous system.

"Watch your thoughts, for they will become actions. Watch your actions, for they will become habits. Watch your habits for they will forge your character. Watch your character, for it will make your destiny".

These formidable words from the former British Prime Minister Margaret Thatcher have always stuck with me, probably because my mother (an Iron Lady in her own right) would echo these words with routine alacrity to her four sons.
It is thought that the original variation of this quote came from the 19th-century English novelist, Charles Reade. Nonetheless, Thatcher understood the importance of linguistics.

Self-talk and the words we use lay down an etching that can have the power to alter our state and emotional wellbeing.

I choose *not* to use the word, hope. The very idea of hope implies that we are waiting on a change of state, an altered state from where we are now. I can not afford to preoccupy myself with a future state with which I (or any of us) have little control over. To hope for change and worry about the future can only lead to anxiety. There is an important distinction here, to ensure we are not in denial of where we are. Rather, with positivity turn our focus towards taking the practical steps that set us free to continue to enjoy a meaningful life.

It is not important if you subscribe to my views here. It is more important that we all be conscious of our own thinking, and choose words (with associated meanings) that resonate for ourselves.

I find it interesting that the ancient practice of Ayurvedic medicine (that is believed to be the oldest system of medicine predating 5,000 years ago) won't use harsh words such as 'disease'. They would instead favour gentler terms such as "You have an *imbalance*" while positively acknowledging there are aspects to work on. For some this might sound like semantics, but I encourage you to think about the words you use and how you describe yourself.

- Be kind to yourself. Adopt language that supports a state of *wellness*.

- Maintain a separation of mind and body.

- Truly embrace change.

- Follow your heart. Remain connected with your inner self.

- Allow emotions to surface and play out.

- Time is subjective. There is no need to rush. Maintain a state of *calm*.

- Find meaning and purpose to your day. You will discover your *happiness*.

- Challenge yourself to new experiences. You will feel *alive* and *invigorated*.

This is wellness.

You are Well.

UBUD, BALI

Nourishing Goodness

Exercise at your own pace. Embrace change.

My running is more of a challenge.
I continue to learn, adapt, and evolve.

Part 3

FOLLOW YOUR PASSIONS

Chapter 11
Adapting & Embracing Change

Throughout this section of the book, we now get to delve a little deeper into the most important part of getting on with life post diagnosis. Learning to adapt and embrace change as we continue to carve out a meaningful life pursuing our passions in some way, shape, or form.

As you read through the following chapters you will notice some recurring themes as to how I like to tackle life head on... no matter what!

- Have confidence in your abilities.

- Try not to let others sway your judgement on what you *should* or *should not* do.

- As we evolve to tune-in and become our *authentic self*, we no longer live a life by the *shoulds*.

- Trust in yourself. You are in the best place to judge your own comfort level and to make wise decisions.

- Have a backup plan and take appropriate precautions.

- Be kind to yourself. It is all good if you need to modify the manner in which you follow your passions.

- Don't judge. Seek to understand.

- Walk tall with an open heart.

- Let go of pride. People are everywhere to help – humanity is very much alive and well.

- Embrace change. Get creative, have fun in the process, stay engaged, maintain connections.

- Allow yourself to be impulsive like there is no tomorrow.

- Continue to explore and challenge yourself. You might be surprised with what you can achieve.

I don't claim to be a practising Buddhist, but I do very much subscribe to the teachings I read.

I especially love the notion of *impermanence,* as per this extract below;

In Buddhism, impermanence (anicca in Pali, anitya in Sanskrit) is one of the three marks of existence, alongside suffering (dukkha) and non-self (anatta). It refers to the fundamental truth that all conditioned phenomena—everything in the universe, including thoughts, emotions, and material objects—are in a constant state of change.

Nothing remains fixed or permanent; everything arises, evolves, and eventually passes away. This includes not only physical objects but also mental states, relationships, and even personal identity. Recognizing impermanence helps reduce attachment and suffering, leading to greater wisdom and liberation from craving and clinging.

For me it has been useful in combining ancient wisdom as we let go of worrying about the future, and draw comfort in the idea that everything that is happening right now is meant to be.

124 BALANCE IN MOTION

Enjoy being present in everything you do, and embrace change!

Photograph: Inspired by the 2020 Netflix series The Queen's Gambit, I dusted off my chess set that was originally given to my father for his 50th birthday. I have a very clear memory as a 15 year old accompanying my mother to pick up this masterpiece from a dutch craftsman in Olinda. Dad taught me chess, and was my first coach for many sports. As I got older and started to beat him at many racquet sports, with a mischievous twinkle in his eyes he would often say, "Son, I will always beat you left-handed at chess".

Could it be that this heirloom has become a metaphor for **embracing change**, as I take joy in having old friends from different walks of life over for dinner, with a challenge to a game of chess, (left-handed).

Chapter 12
Balance & Precision

As a toddler, I recall endless hours riding my Cyclops tricycle doing figure eights 'round and around in the backyard, perfecting precision between the narrow gap of the table tennis table and the verandah pillar. To not be perfect would result in skinned knuckles. This is one of my earliest memories as a 'motion junky' and the need for speed, which developed into a life-long obsession with all things on wheels.

Mother recounts an earlier incidence as a two-year old racing my green tractor up the length of the galley kitchen leaving a line of destruction down the full length of the kitchen cupboards. (Smash up Derby's where all the rage). Then there was the painful bath time scrubbing to remove the (toxic) variety of red and black Texta lines I'd drawn down my arms and legs at four year old kinda, because I wanted to be a Monaro.

Myers Creek to Chum Creek loop, Lake Mountain, Reefton Spur, Highlands, Tolmie to Whitfield, The Snowies (including Granyer Gap and Geehi), threading the eye through the needle with pinpoint accuracy and finding these twisties became my motorcycle playground, demanding perfect balance and precision.

Balance and Parkinson's is an interesting topic and will vary greatly for each individual.

In the bucket of Parkinson's symptoms, you are unlikely to experience every known symptom, and the degree of a symptom may differ greatly.

Hannu Vierikko was a former world champion in dog sledding, who was looking for a way to maintain the training regime for his beloved Huskies during the summer time. After experimenting with harnessing his dogs to his mountain bike, Vierikko hit on the idea of designing and building his own dedicated kick-scooter with a purpose-built harness system for the Huskies to propel him along. In 1994 based in Finland, Vierikko established "Kickbike Worldwide" and arguably became the founder of the modern day scooter phenomenon and competitive racing in Europe. In 2017 I had reason to look for a way to commute to the train station. I purchased a Hannu Vierikko-designed *folding* Kickbike scooter. It is seriously cool as the handlebar collapses down, the frame folds in half, with a short handle protruding at the optimum balance point to allow you to easily pick up the 5.8 kilogram scooter and safely stow behind your seat on the train.

When my neurologist subsequently suggested I could try a walking frame, with a wan smile, I proceeded to talk about my uber cool Kickbike scooter that allows me a high degree of freedom and mobility. I also explained how it could provide a great workout for cross training and core strength while importantly exercising your balance sensory systems. Although my festination is an outcome of a compromised centre of gravity that has me leaning forward (unless I slow down and think through each step), I am thankful that my left-and-right balance is preserved. That allows me to ride two wheels, of all kinds.

A life of being on two wheels combined with 20+ years of yoga I am sure has helped with maintaining neuroplasticity and balance. As I admire my new pot plants in my courtyard, breathing in the early morning fresh air as I do a combination of Qi Gong and Yoga poses, I can hold a tree pose standing on one leg rather well.

Like a scene out of a Bond movie, I land with a flick of the wrist as my self-foiling carbon fibre Komperdell walking poles extend to support my dodgy walking gait, and safeguard against a face plant.
Have fun with technology, give yourself permission to spoil yourself. I love my hi-tech Austrian poles, and are often quick to respond with "It is ski season somewhere in the world", as bemused onlookers watch me do a notional telemark.

Stairs are my friend. "The more difficult the terrain the easier it gets". Sounds like a contradiction, right?
Your midbrain *basal ganglia* is responsible for much of your auto bodily functions such as, blinking, and bladder control. So, too, when you want to get up from your desk to make a coffee, it is your basal ganglia that takes over and allows you to walk to your kitchen bench, with a "Cool, I've got this, I'll take over from here". Whereas, I have to think about every step.

So, why can I dance on the pedals and race my car, catch a ball, run up stairs, and hop across riverstones with agility and control?

I'm at the stage where I can still switch circuitry and use my frontal cortex (executive brain function). This switching ability still doesn't work for everything. My fine motor skills have diminished to a point where I can't play the piano effectively, my writing is laborious, and typing is stilted and slow. And in theory, as those of us with Parkinson's loose more dopamine, the effectiveness of switching will decline. But remember my mantra, "Focus on the here and now, stay present", and challenge yourself on the possibilities of what you can achieve today.

In August 2023 I had no clue as to how I would fare as I hatched a half-baked plan to travel to Vietnam. As I ticked the box for wheel chair assistance (for the first time) at the airports to get through to the gate lounges, I realised how incongruous this was as I would be renting a motorbike to self-ride through the remote highlands between Hoi An and Hanoi.
In the larger cities such as Saigon, I was totally reliant on the "Cyclo" three wheeled taxi bicycles, and Grab taxi scooters to get around. When I asked a Grab scooter driver for directions he was naturally confused when I asked if he could take me there, as I folded my sticks to jump on for the short (ordinarily walkable) 800-metre trip, (balancing with ease, while perched on the back of the scooter with no hand holds).

Precision is no longer the primary objective, balance with control and safety is paramount. As I fit out my shower with hand rails, I am not proud to ask for help and put in measures that I deem are important for me.

Always have your safety in mind and find your own balance between risk and reward.

Work within your own comfort zone, but keep challenging yourself.

Chapter 13
The Plot Thickens

132   BALANCE IN MOTION

With flakey paint, I could just decipher "The Patch", as the green picket gate came crashing down with the blow of a mallet, appropriately like a scaled down wrecking ball from 'Whelan the Wreckers".

I mention Whelan the Wreckers as there is some interesting historical significance of this prominent demolition company on the ground we happen to be standing on, adjacent to the Merri Creek in Brunswick East, an inner suburb of Melbourne.

But to wind back the clock for a bit, Melbourne was established in 1835, and by the 1850s with the advent of the gold rush the city was in a boom economy with much expansion up until the 1880s. Many of the early landmark buildings where modelled on English architecture with the foundations using bluestone. Bluestone is actually a basalt rock formed by ancient volcanic activity that produced extensive lava flows. These vast basalt plains extend west and southwest of my home state of Victoria, and are said to be amongst the largest basalt plains in the world. With demand for construction for roads, curbing, bridges, buildings (beyond just base foundations), bluestone became a prominent building material. It is said that the early sailing ships returning empty to mother England used to take onboard bluestone blocks as a means to provide ballast.

So back to the land we are standing on alongside the Merri Creek, this area was one of the early bluestone quarries. In fact, about 300 metres from where I live are the remnants of the base of a 'derrick crane' which consisted of a mast, boom, and hoisting mechanism. Once you dig a big hole, invariably they need to be filled up again. Towards the turn of the last century,

THE PLOT THICKENS

Melbourne was undergoing another wave of transformation, as the company Whelan the Wrecker established their original operations in Albert Street, Brunswick. They were contracted to demolish many of the early Victorian era buildings. Much of the rubble ended up in the old quarries. When the quarry in Brunswick closed in the early 1970s, it also became a tip.

Let us jump to 1982 when a bunch of local enterprising environmentalists approached the then Brunswick council to secure a rent-free lease on the four hectares of land which by now was a disused tip (the former quarry), with an ambition to restore the land and create a model for sustainability and urban farming. An initial 10-year lease was signed as locals joined forces to make good of the land and establish a community garden. It resulted into what became the early formation of CERES (Centre for Education and Research in Environmental Strategies).

CERES today has become an outstanding success in education, in showcasing environmental and sustainability concepts with more than 65,000 students visiting each year. In addition to that, the organisation provides many short courses and workshops conducted on topics such as permaculture design, urban farming and bee keeping. With over half a million visitors each year, from its humble beginnings over 40 years ago, it has become a model for social enterprise with cafes, organic grocery, bakery, a market garden (in addition to the community garden plots), a retail nursery and fair wood enterprise. Operating as a not-for-profit, it gives back to the community and society as a whole, delivering on the positive message "**For people to fall in love with the Earth again**".

In August 2021, we had a two-week window to help with the demolition of the almost 40-year old original community garden plots, to make way for a renewal project for a new community garden hub offering broader community engagement and accessibility. I had got involved with the demolition as a volunteer with no expectations as to what would eventuate. To my surprise, for my efforts, I was offered a rather nice corner plot.

We gained access to the new plots in February 2022 as 45 eager and excited families (plot owners) came together to do the final preparation before planting. Many close relationships were formed on that first working bee where we had to hand wheelbarrow the rich soil into each plot. It is interesting for me to have this timestamp when I had the coordination to wheelbarrow more than 40 heavy soil laden barrows, in addition to loading by hand-shovel, countless other barrows.

My plot had a slight fall to the pathway, so I started to think through some permaculture ideas. I wanted to make sure I could do some deep watering. Therefore, I came up with the idea of a one metre length piece of (100 millimetres in diameter) drainage pipe and proceeded to drill hole's on the lower one third. Determining the high point of the garden plot, I inserted the pipe 400 millimetres into the ground to create a central point for deep watering (knowing that our new garden soil was still on top of a hard base). I knew that I would plant rosemary and lavender on the low side, as their root system would help provide structure to help retain water within the plot. Additionally I wanted to add a trench. Ultimately, my trench had a dual purpose for water channeling but also a central walkway. I started to carve a channel following the lay of the land. As I stood back to survey my handy work, it suddenly occurred to me I had pretty much formed the shape of a *question mark*. I raced over to our stock pile to find a bluestone block to use as the dot to complete my question mark.

Feeling very happy, with my question mark which became an all encompassing metaphor.

- Do we really own this land, or are we custodians entrusted to protect it?
- Are we living light on this plant?
- What can I do to ensure a more sustainable future? How can I reduce my own environmental impact?

The question mark became a vehicle for much thoughtful pondering.

The annual mega working-bee sessions retrospectively became an interesting litmus test to my Parkinson's progression. In February 2023, with increased festination, I struggled to control my run-away wheel barrow with just one light load of mulch.

By February 2024 I was finding it increasingly difficult to weed, til the soil and plant seedlings. My fellow plot owners provided caring assistance as my fine motor skills and coordination declined.

I made the decision to relinquish my plot in October 2024 for several reasons. With the warmer weather arriving, for over a year now I'd struggled with running or walking the 600 metres to the plot to water daily.
Increasingly, I had become reliant on my uber cool folding manual kick scooter to get around. Dealing with the harvest became a concern as I struggled to prepare my produce, with the chopping and cutting.

As at February 2025 I finally decided to get some home assistance to help with the meal prep cutting. It is quite a luxury (and fun) to have a prep chef in your own kitchen doing all the hard work while I get to play celebrity head chef as I pull my prepared ingredients out of the fridge and star in my own cooking show. :-)

I'd had three wonderful years of personal growth and connection. It was a logical point in time for the plot to go to another family who could be more productive (knowing that the waitlist to secure a plot was over 100 registered applicants). I had learnt and contributed in many ways. Giving up the plot was not giving up the community.

Of the many events and festivals, amongst my favourite activities I still get to enjoy are the annual Harvest Festival, The Winter Solstice Festival, and Olives to Oil (an annual festival where you can bring your own olives along to contribute to a communal pressing). Whenever I am at a loose end, I can often be seen at the Saturday morning market catching up with local stall holders who have become personal friends, and as I wander up to the cafe to listen to live music. The cafe music hub creates a supportive environment that fosters the up-and-coming beautiful young talent, playing a variety of music from soulful jazz, folk, classical and the occasional Irish fiddlers, and more.

The local relationships we cultivate will flourish and return such care and support.

Chapter 14
Carlo Abarth

As the new kid on the block, I diligently unscrewed the button on my handbrake as instructed. With a group walk to orient ourselves of the first days Motorkhana 'test', the more experienced hands provided tips on how to achieve a fast time. It was 1982, at a time when our car club had access to a paddock outside the small farming town of Athlone in East Gippsland. With a front wheel drive car, often the fastest way around a flag (or cone) is to take a tight line and momentarily tweak the handbrake to slide the rear out, and in doing so, point the car in the right direction as you line up the next flag. For many other flag markers, you are often best to loop the flags and maintain your momentum and speed. With a burst of noise we head for the home garage being careful not to hit the hay-bales.

Motorkhana's are not only a professional sport globally, but at a car club level provides a great environment for new drivers and kids from 13 years onwards to gain invaluable experience and finesse for car control. On a competition day, there might be up to six or more different tests (layouts) to be memorised. Going around just one flag the wrong way will incur a WD (wrong direction), with the stop watch immediately stopped, and with no time recorded for the run. Knocking over a flag/cone will incur a time penalty. I soon developed a reputation for accuracy and had many events with no WDs.

In April 2019, I decided to reconnect with the club as I planned a transition from two wheels to purchasing a

CARLO ABARTH

four-wheel sports car. I had come to watch the 'Nationals', an annual three day event. For this season it was held at *The Bend*, just outside of Adelaide complete with its own trackside hotel. For car buffs it has the best hotel foyer in the world, comprising of a multi-million dollar private collection of high-end exotica including Ferrari, Lamborghini, McLaren, and Porsche.

Although I was there to watch, on day three, I was offered a drive of a friends "Special" (a purpose built motorkhana car, complete with "fiddle brakes" that allow you to vary the brake bias to the front, rear or just one side). My late entrance was accepted so I started to try and commit to memory the various tests for the day.

In unison, when the onlookers see someone do a WD, they immediately look away, so as not to confuse or jinx themselves for their own run. The crowds looked away on every one of my runs. How could this be? OK, it had been a few decades since my last motorkhana, and I didn't think being in a friend's car was a valid excuse (even though it was a brute to drive). After all, I was the master of never getting WDs.

So the truth is, I was year one into my Parkinson's diagnosis. An early symptom for many Parky's is *foggy brain*. In at least the final three years of my work life I had been masking foggy brain. At no point did it ever make me unsafe to drive per se, (my cognition thankfully has always been preserved), but there is no question I had feelings of disorientation as I tried to recall from memory the intricate, overlapping patterns as I attempted to drive the motorkhana test.

There is some further context and exciting outcomes to all of this. You'll recall that it was 2020 that I commenced an anti-inflammatory focus to my nutrition. I can report that foggy-brain is a symptom I have absolutely reversed. In early 2024, I was involved in a Parkinson's study at LaTrobe where I performed in the upper end of the range (of the general population).

It was actually quite an interesting study with the hypothesis that eye movement could be used as an early marker for Parkinson's. Participants were hooked up to some interesting eye sensory equipment that would plot and record our eye movement as we responded to stimuli and cognitive tasks.

Carlo Abarth was an Austrian racer, who eventually took up Italian citizenship having established an automotive performance tuning company "Abarth & C." in 1949 in Turin. Abarth soon built a reputation for hotting up Porsches, Alfas and Fiats in particular. In July 1971, Fiat acquired Abarth, and to this day, Abarth remains the performance arm of Fiat, providing limited high-performance variants of Fiats under the Abarth brand.

In February 2020, I was lucky enough to purchase one of the last new Abarth modern day classics, styled off the original 1966 open top, two door 124 Spider, as I completed my objective to get back onto the racetrack, attending a few club days.

As I approach the high-speed right-hander with heart in mouth as you momentarily lift off the go pedal to float through the corner, then stomp back on the pedal with full noise as you sight the apex. As you approach Southern Loop, it is important to take an initial midline and not come in too soon as it is a double radius corner, requiring you to aim at the second (true) apex. Keep in tight and you will gain time as you breath deeply under full power to take the long left hand sweeper of Stoner Corner. With the ball of your foot firmly planted on the brake pedal, you rotate your foot to blip the accelerator with your heal (in a technique called 'healing and toeing'), to ensure you match revs (engine speed) to road speed, as I grabbed third gear from sixth (while under heavy braking). Phillip Island Circuit is without a doubt one of the best race tracks and certainly the most picturesque in the world.

I feel fortunate that I've had five awesome years with this car and the new and old friendships formed through automotive pursuits.

In April 2025, I had the opportunity to attend a practice day at the lesser known Bryant Park hill climb. I was super happy with my lines and pinpoint accuracy for a track I had never driven previously. As I write, I am totally OK with the idea that this may well be my last outing on a track, and as I consider selling my beloved Abarth for something more practical (as I struggle to get in and out). I'm excited by technology, and are rather interested in something 'E', with all the passive safety gear such as adaptive cruise control, and emergency autonomous braking.

Daunting to consider that I have had a connection with car clubs (off and on) for over 40 years.

I feel eternally grateful for the long-term friendships and associations. Enduring friendships that increasingly provide such wonderful care, compassion and support.

Chapter 15
Music Is For Life

As I toss and turn, now fully awake, through squinty eyes I register that it is just after midnight. The clouds are mostly obscured by the darkness of the night, but as the street light filters through the lounge room sheers, I feel compelled to get up. As if by levitation, I'm now sitting at my piano with the formation of a tune cycling through my head. I simply had to record it. Such can be the pull of creative pursuits.

It was April of 2023. As I played around with some dark and moody descending tones in G minor, I hit the record button and laid down an initial 16 bars of a piece I later called "Intrigo dal Cielo Oscuro" (Intrigue from the Obscure Sky).

The following month, visiting up from Tasmania to play a gig at Paris Cat was my dear friend and wonderfully talented pianist Ade Ishs. With great enthusiasm, Ade sat down to help me finish it off by writing the C section. He then opened up his laptop to transcribe it and create a Jazz chart in an electronic publishing tool. Such is the generosity of not only Ade, but of the local Jazz community I feel blessed to be part of.

Ade, an infinitely more accomplished pianist, brought life into our collaboration in a manner well beyond my skill, and kindly debuted this piece at a regional jazz festival, along with performances at Paris Cat and other major events. Vincent Bradley captures the very essence of this piece with his interpretations, creating a most expressive and haunting intrigue, made possible by the mesmerising sounds of his flugelhorn, with Lachlan Wallace on drums and Paul Bonnington on bass adding their magic.

MUSIC IS FOR LIFE 147

In 2010, I had bought a piano with the mission to learn the elements of jazz improvisation, building upon my classical training several decades earlier. I had some wonderful mentors in Steve Sedergreen, Dan Robertson (now residing back in New Zealand), Adam Rudegeair, and a number of other characters who are committed to supporting local grassroots jazz through facilitating Open Mic jazz jams, (with special thanks to Kevin Blaze and Ann Craig who gave me my first foray into playing publicly).

By February of 2020 at a jazz jam in St Kilda, it was my turn to solo. This was the first time I experienced a Parkinson's-related glitch while playing as my right arm became completely wooden and I was unable to run my hand up the keyboard.

My writing had been affected a couple of years earlier, but now my continued loss of fine motor skills increasingly impacts a number of daily tasks.
Best not to ask me to slice a loaf of bread as I struggle with the whole sawing action. Oh, and I often have friends cut up my steak.

But none of this is doom and gloom. Living in the epicentre of inner Melbourne, the music capital of Australia, I get to hang out at a myriad of jazz clubs within a two kilometre radius and support live music[1].

Learning jazz improvisation could be likened to doing a fine wine appreciation course. I now have the language, the vocabulary that provides a deeper understanding for my taste in jazz. I have a more meaningful experience as an active listener, with a better appreciation of the building blocks for improvisation, chord constructs, and jazz voicings. Give me a flat fifth any day with a suspended 11th (that replaces the third with a fourth to create some tension).

Tension in jazz is like chewing on a sour power. With sensors overloaded from the initial bite, "Do I like this"? Should this resolve into something more familiar, or will it linger? Jazz is about tantalising the audience, stretching the listener's ears.

Within 10 minutes of being in a performance jazz club environment, it is interesting to see my right hand tremor completely calm as my mind locks into the rhythm of jazz (especially if a pianist is on stage).

Speaking of the mind and curiously for me, I happened to read Oliver Sacks, "Musicophilia", a couple of years before he passed away in August 2015. Sacks was a neurologist and writer who lived in New York City where he was a professor of neurology and psychiatry at Columbia University. In his book Musicophilia he describes with absolute compassion the intriguing accounts of music on the human condition. Of note is a chapter titled "Kinetic Melody: Parkinson's Disease and Music Therapy", where he recounts some extraordinary stories of the therapeutic benefits of music. Sacks also draws upon references to his earlier book titled "Awakenings" (which was adapted into the 1990 film by the same name starring Robin Williams as Dr Oliver Sacks, and Robert De Niro as one of the patients). In the 1960s while Sacks was a physician at the Beth Abraham Hospital, he got to meet one of the early pioneers of music therapy and witness the extraordinary work of Kitty Stiles.

As I reread excerpts from Musicophilia, I'm reminded of the power of dance and specifically Argentine Tango. On page 280, Sacks notes that, *"Argentine Tango is a dance done in an embrace or frame, unlike swing or salsa. This aspect is particularly useful to individuals who are challenged in terms of balance, because the partner may provide helpful sensory information and stabilizing support that leads to improved balance and gait"*.

At a recent friends wedding as I ditched my walking poles and slowly managed my festination shuffling onto the dance floor, I was ecstatic to be able to sneak in a credible dance routine with the bride... :-)

Music is for life.

Keep dancing to the beat!

---

1. *"The daily rituals of life should be celebrated... acknowledging the everyday rituals, you will find happiness"*

   With these gentle words, **Mina Yu** provides her personal insights behind the release of her new album *"A Day and Life"* (June 2025).

Chapter 16
Come Stai

M *i piace andare in bicicletta in montagna con gli amici.*

There was little convincing required for my two Italian friends (who are avid adventurers), to rise to the challenge of hurtling down the relatively new Cascades Trail, an epic 28-kilometre mountain bike trail that descends from the summit of Lake Mountain (1.5 hours east of Melbourne) into Marysville (a small picturesque village in the foothills).

It is an exhilarating 1,550-metre descent full of berms (steep fast flowing banked turns), with plenty of *black-diamond* fly-overs for the brave hearted. For self preservation though, I always opt for the *blue-diamond* bi-pass (I'm not that foolhardy, and I do know my limits).
"Oh, there are some bits uphill", the Park Ranger casually remarked, but stopped short of mentioning that there is actually a combined 500 metres of ascent (hold on to this thought for a moment).

So, it was in March 2023 when we attempted this ride. The significance of 2023 is that The Kona Bicycle Company had just released their 20th anniversary version of their legendary 'Unit'. Legendary because in 2003 Kona was the first to mass produce a stripped back, hardcore minimalist, *single-speed* mountain bike. You read 'single-speed' correctly, and as I was now a proud owner of said anniversary model, you could well imagine the mild concern of ascents – after all, this was supposed to be a downhill trail, right!

In the final sector of this trail there is a massively steep descent of 800 metres in less than three kilometres. Within the first corner, I had stop to lower my seat, to alleviate the very real risk of catapulting over the handlebars. The 'arm-pump' generated by gravity was numbing. I had no choice but to push through. The decision to wear my full face helmet, knee pads, and arm pads proved to be wise. With minimal funding for maintenance, the trails fall into disrepair. It was late in the season, the high side of the berms where breaking, combined with much debris, boulders and corrugated erosion. Needless to say I bailed off the bike a few times.

To clarify, the Kona Unit is not only a single speed, but also is a heavy steel frame without any suspension at all (rigid frame). It also has reasonably standard 60 millimetre (2.3 inch) wide tyres.

If we discount 'fat bikes' which are a style of bike with massive ballon tyres that are designed to provide a degree of cushioning (replacing the need for suspension), odds are on that, I still hold the record for anyone silly enough to attempt the Cascades Trail on a single speed, rigid frame mountain bike. Made all the more insane knowing that I also own a lightweight carbon fibre, full suspension mountain bike, that is ideally suited for the Cascades Trail.

The truth is I picked my way through slowly, proving the point that you can achieve an awful lot if you put your mind to it. It did help having the wonderful camaraderie of my friends who were very patient with my lack of pace, and were hugely supportive strapping me onto the saddle and pushing me down the hill. ;-)

There is a back story as to why I purchased the Kona Unit. The end game was to build this bike up as a (geared) bike-packing bike, better suited for carrying my camp gear and supplies, to do multi day touring along Victoria's historic rail trails. My LaPierre carbon fibre full suspension mountain bike lacks the frame space to properly store gear, and having to pedal all day wearing a backpack is tiresome.

In 2021, I had this growing awareness that my body was slowing down, even though it had been an awesome year with two major solo hiking expeditions. I was determined to ensure I would keep enjoying the Australian outdoors, and the wonderful grounding effect (beyond the literal sense) of camping out *in harmony with mother nature.*

By the end of 2021, I'd accomplished my first ever bike-packing tour, riding my mountain bike along the Mansfield to Tallarook rail trail. I went the long way 'round to the head of the trail at Mansfield.
With the bike stowed safely on the regional country train from the Southern Cross Station, I got to speak to some locals who suggested I could set up camp around the back of the horse racing track, that was five minutes away from our train destination in Benalla (central Victoria).

When you are independent with camp gear, you can afford to wing it, and just as well that I packed my tent as there was a festival that weekend with zero accommodation available. The joy of expeditions is in the planning and preparation. Although

having to wear a backpack for clothing and food is never ideal, overall, I was rather pleased with my set-up. I had only made two purchases to augment the gear I already owned:
1) An Ortlieb waterproof handlebar *roll bag*, and 2) a new style of ultra light-weight and compact *sleeping quilt*, (about 30% lighter than a conventional sleeping bag – but take care to watch the weather as sleeping quilts are a compromise and are only rated for three seasons).

Miraculously my handlebar roll bag only weighed precisely two kilograms including contents of: sleeping quilt, marino thermo liner, air mattress, air pillow, Whisper Light tent, my beautifully crafted Japanese Asoto titanium stove set, and butane canister.

> *Problem solving, improvising, getting creative, is what it's all about. Ploughing in deep and going for it.*

Up and over the remote Mount Samaria State Park, you really don't want to have a mechanical failure out here as this is off the beaten track without a soul around.

As I reached the Midland Highway, it was tempting to stop along side the Nillahcootie Dam. The morning sunrise filtering through the hovering mist across the dam would have been magical, but I decided to push on to Mansfield for a much needed pub meal, hot shower and bed.

With my cog-wheel gait rigidity in my right leg, I can no longer spin at pace. Accordingly I tend to be very quad dominant as I grind my way in a low gear. Albeit Mount Samaria was a killer to pick your way through, this was only a 72-kilometre ride. However, my pace is way down with an elapsed 8.5 hours in the saddle, arriving into town just after dusk.

At the time of writing, January of 2022 was to be my last bike-packing (four-day, three-night) cycling expedition, along the southern half of the infamous 'Goldfields Track' from Castlemaine to Buninyong.
The Goldfields track is steeped in history, going back to Victoria's gold rush of the 1850s. The Chinese miners where a tough and resilient bunch. To save on port entry fees at Melbourne, many elected to disembark at Adelaide and walk for several weeks to the goldfields in central Victoria. Many of the Chinese established their communities along the Goldfields track, where you can see remnants of much innovation they introduced to mining, such as:

1. The ***water wheel***, to extract gold more efficiently from the tailings.

2. ***Water races***, which are a combination of stone walled channels and ditches to direct water from nearby

streams.

3. **Sluices,** which are long narrow boxes with trays, that were designed to separate out the heavier gold from the lighter soil.

I traverse the environment with total fascination for the history before me.

The catalyst for this bike-packing trip was to arrive in Buninyong and to pay witness to gold in its refined form of a medallion with the inscription, *"2022 Road Cycling National Championships".* Specifically I'd come to the Nationals to cheer on Australia's inspirational multi gold medalist Paralympian Carol Cooke as she competed in the para-criterium.

A year earlier, I'd struck up a conversation with Carol, when I was totally intrigued to see this hi-tech tricycle approaching my local cafe on the Inner Circle Railway bike path. We had a wonderful meeting of minds as we geeked out on the technical aspects of her bike. Carol has multiple sclerosis, but our physical *differences* did not really factor into our conversation, beyond a fleeting acknowledgement. We did however touch on the idea of randomness. Was our meeting perchance? Do connections happen from some higher state of consciousness?

So, my 2023 Kona has yet to see an overnight cycle tour, but two years later I am now adapting to the idea of replacing it with an electric gravel bike.

The title of this chapter, "How are you" in Italian, has been somewhat deliberately misleading. Apart from the fact that my usual response to this question is to say, "Fine". And I don't mean to say FINE in a way that our adorable petulant teenage kids might say (with hands clasped behind back, rocking from side to side), when we know something is troubling them.

I truly mean I am fine. I am the happiest I have ever been in my life.

This chapter has been about community and connections made through following your passions, and adapting to change – resulting in a wonderful sense of contentment and happiness.

Speaking of community, in my opening sentence I referred to two 'Italian' friends, which is stretching the truth somewhat. You see, none of us are Italian. In fact one is from Belgium. The other one is as Aussie as I am.

Whilst on a quest to maintain my neuroplasticity, I had decided to enrol in Italian lessons, which is where we *tre amici* had met.

With many other beautiful friendships formed through Italian classes, and our collective obsession with all things Italian. Although I stopped formal lessons after two years, we remain a tight knit group catching up for coffee in Lygon Street, Italian festivals, the occasional dinners (Italian of course), the annual Italian Film Festival, Italian gallery exhibitions and more.

Ultimately, my very dear bunch of friends from Italian studies is a great example of my concept of **"Lily pads of communities"** that sometimes intersect with other common interests such as; mountain biking, Formula One, classic cars, Australian Open, jazz, art, travel, and food. Speaking of food, we have been known to scour Melbourne's finest authentic biscotteria's to find the best Neapolitan pastry *sfogliatelle* – totally decadent with layers of flakey pastry, shaped like a shell, filled with ricotta, semolina, and citrus zest.

Si, è bellissimo

(Now how does this fit with an anti-inflammatory focus on foods, I hear you say? Be kind to yourself, allow yourself to digress).

Enjoy expanding your community of interests.

Va tutto bene!

Chapter 17
Going Solo

South Coast Wilderness Track, Tasmania

After a quick fly over to confirm the condition of our alarmingly short gravel airstrip at Melaleuca, my pilot made the final ascent in our three seater plane to drop me off in one of the most remote parts of the south coast wilderness in Tasmania. A grade 5 hike, the highest grading of difficulty recommended for experienced bushwalkers with navigation and first aid skills.

"Head south young man and you'll find the trail head. Keep going... Good luck", came the final words of encouragement (well at least, I took his comments in the positive).
It was now 4:30 pm, much later than originally planned. With an approximate four hour hike to my first nights camp at Cox Bight, timing would be tight knowing that the sunset was due around 9:00 pm.

This had been our second attempt to fly out of Cambridge Aerodrome (northeast of Hobart). After an early rise to catch the 8:30 am flight operated by Par Avion, we had such a picturesque flight over the Derwent River. With ominous clouds ahead as we traversed the coastal route above water between Bruny Island and the mainland, my pilot thought it was prudent to go into a holding pattern before attempting to head through the Southwest mountain ranges. Light aircraft are very much designed for fair-weather conditions for optimum safety. As the winds picked up, we were starting to get quite buffeted around with a growing sense of unease as to how vulnerable we were in our tin-can with wings and a single prop. With clear blue skies behind us and a black wall approaching at a furious rate, there was no need to convince me that we had to return to base, as the wiper blades (reminiscent of a 1959 Mini) struggled to keep up from the now pelting rain.

We travel for the unexpected

Embrace the unexpected

The hike proper had not begun, yet I was already immersed in a most wonderful adventure full of twists and turns (quite literally), testing our resilience. I had just had the most epic added bonus of an unscheduled personal scenic flight.
Does it really matter that I'd been up since 6:00 am? Now back at the aerodrome, I was faced with the uncertainty of the weather not clearing in time to allow for a flight out (within the last available window prior to 3:30 pm).

Now was the time to conserve energy and not stress out – it is likely to be a very long day. Rest, meditate, stay hydrated, well nourished, and prepare (mentally and physically for the possibility of a late flight out (which thankfully, did eventuate).

Hiking expeditions over many years had taught me that hiking is more of a mental game rather than the physical – I had intuitively been practicing mindfulness for some time.

A Tipping Point

The decision to embark on an epic solo expedition for eight days was quite intentional. It spanned over 85 kilometres through some of the toughest terrain in absolute wilderness of the South Coast Track. As I prepared for this expedition in the January of 2021, I could already sense that I was starting to struggle with the pace of my regular hike group.

By February 2022 my self assessment came to bear during a group hike through the central plateau of Tasmania in an area called the '1000 Lakes', and more specifically, The Walls of Jerusalem. With my regular hike buddies, we were a party of eight, traversing an undefined southern loop section off compass, before heading northwest to join the defined track.

Day 1 was to be a fairly straightforward 14 kilometre walk honing our orientation skills under compass.
At around the 10 kilometre mark, I experienced a lack of orientation of a very different kind. With the soft button grass coming to the rescue I experienced my first ever neurological fall. I then struggled on to make the final four kilometres, and the team had to help me set up my tent, fetch water from a nearby stream, and cook up my dinner. It was early to bed, with allowances for a later start the next day. The team rallied to reroute the expedition that would give us a two night base camp at Lake Ball.

So, I was able to rationalise and understand the factors that related to my neurological hiccup. This hike was at year 4 since diagnosis and I had yet to fully understand what would exacerbate symptoms. We had flown the previous afternoon from Melbourne to Hobart to stay in a shared house. Having walked a few kilometres into town that night for a pub meal at the local mariner, spirits were high in anticipation.

Late to bed upon a pullout stretcher in the lounge wasn't ideal. We are all different – some like to wake up to the news and TV ads blaring. I am used to stillness and calm. Our driver had arrived at 8:00 am for our 4.5 hour drive to our drop-off point where we would commence our hike. We forget how noisy old Toyota HiAce vans are, combined with the exuberant chatter. My noise cancelling headphones didn't quite cut the mustard.

The picture I'm attempting to paint here is one of neurological overload, (and definitely not being mean spirited towards my dear friends). The reality is over stimuli had become increasingly difficult to deal with.

Neurological overload and stimuli, requires a deeper explanation and will no doubt differ for others with Parkinson's.

In my earlier chapter. 'At One...', you will recall the meditative qualities I experience as a motorcyclist. I can still ride all day without feeling fatigued, as I singularly engage in the joy of riding, (stimulating the senses as the kaleidoscope of vibrant scenery pour through my visor).

(In August of 2023, I rented a Honda 125 cc trail motorbike for nine days and self guided through the central highlands of Vietnam from Hoi An to Hanoi).

In stark contrast, examples of over stimuli include:

- The intensity I experience in just an hour and a half of an Italian lesson is extremely draining on the senses, and I come away feeling fatigued.

- I find multiple group conversations (especially with background noise), increasingly overwhelming. I much prefer to be more present in 1:1 catchups. I do recognise that this is not unique and that many would relate to this. However, I am more referring to over-stimuli, neurological overload that exacerbates symptoms.

- With caring intentions when my friends tried to spur me along on that final 4 kilometres of our hike, I was offered music, conversation to keep me going, "Here, follow my steps". I had to carefully explain that what I needed was total silence and space, and reassured them that left to my own pace I would get there.

- I briefly touched on my nine day motorcycle adventure through the remote interior of Vietnam. We had in fact left Hoi An with three other mates. On day 4 I made the decision to go solo. Again I stress this is no indictment on my dear friends. It was very much a positive self awareness that I needed to; run to my own rhythm, set my own pace, stop when my body said so, hydrate, rest, wake up when I wanted to, not have to keep track of fellow riders, eat when I needed to, and go with the flow.

I really enjoy navigating, and it is less of a neurological overload when you are not responsible for your fellow riders. Without trying to sound selfish, I do just have to protect my neuron's to ensure I am safe and can get through the day – your caring friends will understand. Perhaps ironically, I really thrive in the big cities such as Hanoi where it took me 1.5 hours from the outskirts of the city to my central hotel through the totally exhilarating congestion and mayhem created by crater-sized pot holes, trucks and buses with their musical horns (of reassurance), whole families on scooters, mothers breastfeeding on the back of scooters, kids on scooters, almost universally scooters without mirrors (mirrors are too wide to cut through the traffic), commercial scooters heavily ladened and precariously wide, bicycles, cars, chooks, dogs, a mass of people crossing, street vendors, hand carts, tri-bicycle carts, and rain.

I'm still not quite sure why I am able to remain so calm in what otherwise is a mass of external stimuli, but I think it has something to do with being singularly focused doing something I love, and in a zen like state engaging the pineal gland (third eye).

Now back to January 2021 and my solo hike through the toughest hike I have ever done, the South Coast Wilderness Track. I knew what my body was capable of, and I was developing some awareness in knowing how to manage/avoid excessive stimuli and neurological overload.

Have confidence in your ability, take appropriate precautions, and go for it!

There are at least three critical areas to be aware of along the South Coast Wilderness Track:

> 1. On day 3, the 900 metre ascent of Iron Mountain Range with its rocky escarpment is too dangerous to attempt without clear visibility. Often under a cloud of cover, I was blessed with sunshine. Mountains can be highly changeable within a nanosecond. I chose to make a hasty beat across the exposed summit as the roaring southerlies kept me at a rakish angle.
> I'd been navigating for a few kilometres, so was relieved when I picked up a trail marker, and retreated to the tree line for lunch, before continuing the long descent through the rainforest of tangled roots through knee deep bog, which made the going tough into Little Deadman's Bay.
>
> 2. Leaving Little Deadman's Bay for Prion Beach, you have to be aware of the tide changes as there is one section that is only passable at low tide – bush bashing inland around the point is not really an option. (Less critical, but best to also do Granite Beach at low tide, as the

beach sand is far more pleasant than the otherwise granite boulders at high tide.)

3. Have you ever experienced a *three boat river crossing system?*
The bushwalking code is to ensure that at least one boat is always available on each bank.
So, if you arrive at the New River Lagoon crossing to find just one boat on your side, you have to:

- Row your boat to the other bank (where there will be two boats).

- Tie one boat to your boat, and proceed to tow this spare boat back to the river bank whence you came.

- Drop off the spare boat and continue back across the river in your original intended crossing.

The concept sounds easy enough, right! The mouth of the New River Lagoon is wide (very wide), flat and subject to tidal changes. Parks Tasmania, have provided some highly appropriate seaworthy aluminium dinghies, fit for the occasion (but read... Heavy). With flat sandy banks, expect to have to drag said dinghy some 10 to 20 metres to waters edge.
As per above scenario, that's potentially three crossings, heavily laden, against constant tidal flow.

I'm a solo hiker, how was that going to work?

I arrived safely at Cockle Creek, my final destination on day 7, with one spare day up my sleeve.

Sitting on the back step of Rose and Walter Adams delightful 1930s blue washed timber cottage with its multiple small square panes of white windows overlooking Rocky Bay.
A most wonderful day of rest and recuperation, splashing about with naked abandonment in this most pristine paradise.

Sealed up since 2003, I placed my hands on the well worn brass door handle and tried to imagine the life these two shared in peaceful isolation, who became Australia's most southern residents from 1947 when the Heather Family Sawmill closed. Walter died in 1967, with Rose staying on in their cottage for another 35 years.

The plaque reads,

"It was beautiful and quiet – I'd go fishing and chop wood and look after myself and everyone else around the place – all the walkers that used to get lost used to come to my place"

So, this chapter was not about being single, living with Parkinson's, but I will offer this perspective.

As a solo adventurer (in life's broader journey), you connect with people more deeply, even if for a fleeting moment.

To illustrate this point, I'll provide a travel example. Whilst on the South Coast Track there was only a handful of hikers I saw the entire time. Tom and his three mates had managed to catch a king sized crab at Little Deadman's Bay, and proceeded to generously include me in the feast. The next morning they had left early. As I walked along Prion beach, I headed over the low dune, through grass tussocks to the boat crossing at New River Lagoon, to be warmly greeted by Tom and his mates. You see they had already realised the gravity of the situation and had waited for me, (having already gone across to retrieve the spare boat). As I gratefully slumped into the dinghy, we all sang, "Don't pay the ferryman...", as the burly ex footballers took turns to row against the strong tide.

I feel blessed to have experienced much travel and adventure.

With common alacrity, I'm often asked, "Are you alone".

My standard reply is, "Solo, but never alone".

Chapter 18
Soar to New Heights

A Versatile Tourer, with Panache

May 2021

"Groan... Oh no, do you really expect me to fit in there... Really?"

Never heard my Deuter pack complain so much, and considering I was the one who would be lugging said pack up the infamous Hannels Spur over the coming two days, pack doth protest too much!

So the challenge and destination was to climb Australia's highest ascent from Geehi Flats campground up 2,200 metres to the summit of Kosciusko in sub-zero conditions, following the first big dumping of snow in the Australian alps.

The 124 Spider is wonderfully versatile. Happy to cruise the Hume, and comes into its own with panache as the corners tighten on the B400 towards my first night's base camp.

Near the Tintaldra turn off, I get my first glimpse of snow capped mountains. With mixed emotions, I contemplate the sanity of my solo expedition. Have I judged the weather patterns correctly? (The Main Ridge can be miserable.) Mental checklist of gear. Yep, I've packed my 'beam me up Scottie' locator beacon.

The decision to buy a two door ragtop can bring some mild anxiety, as we consider if it will suit our every need. (Perhaps a similar anxiety to those pondering 'e' vehicles, with the ever-present fear of running out of charge).

SOAR TO NEW HEIGHTS

Over the past 1.5 years of ownership, I found the 124 Spider to be the most versatile, capable, and fun care I've owned. Golf clubs are a challenge but doable. Ikea runs are hilarious, and now camping expeditions are perfect with a snuggly fitted pack stowed.

For us motorcyclists, the Snowy's provides some of the best riding roads. The section from Khancoban to Geehi is always a favourite, and on this occasion provided equal delight in the opened top four wheeler, and reconfirmed my decision to take the Spider.

With half-cover installed, the 124 survived the overnight low of minus 2 degrees celsius.
Time to wade across the icy waters of the Swampy Plains River to find the head of Hannels Spur 'track' just north of Dr Forbes Hut (it was a rare moment having to use a GPS to locate the starting line). Within 50 metres the long ascent began steadily upwards to Morias Flats campsite, and at 1,528 metres, it offered the first drifts of snow.

Absolutely blessed with weather. After an overnight low of minus 4 degrees celsius, the skies were clear and sunny without a breath of wind in the air, which made for a perfect summit. With an almost full moon and knowledge of the elevated boardwalk from summit to Thredbo, I had the most magnificent sunset followed by a moonlit walk back to the Thredbo Chairlift. Then I walked down the Village ski run under head torch to the welcoming shimmering lights of the Thredbo Alpine Village Hotel bar.

In 2020, I started writing the occasional special-interest articles for my Italian car club magazine, ostensibly in recognition that many of our club members shared other passions beyond four wheels.

Beyond the extract of the article above, there is a deeper story to be told from a Parkinson's perspective.

*At the time of this hike, I had not been taking bioceuticals (supplements) and was yet to fully understand some fairly common **deficiencies**, and **malabsorptions** associated with Parkinson's, even though I was aware of the known correlation between microbiome (gut health) and neurological conditions. I soon got to learn about Integrated General Practitioners who adopt a more holistic approach. There are private laboratories that can provide a variety of in-depth, targeted blood and urine tests.*

Working in with an Integrated GP to obtain as much baseline data as early into your journey, I personally believe, is worthwhile (ideally at point of diagnosis), and it can help you build out a supplements plan based on measured deficiencies.

I was still experiencing the occasional restless leg syndrome at night, and experiencing leg cramps. On day one of this hike, I was mildly concerned as to whether I would make it to Morias Flats campsite. There is a reason why the Australian army are said to have used this route for training. As Australia's highest ascent, it is brutal and relentless. Within a few hundred metres my quads and calfs were burning and cramping up big time. No need to panic. I was hiking solo, so there was no pressure, and I knew I could walk within my own limits. The worst case scenario was that I could down my pack and set up tent in the middle of the track, if my legs failed to behave. Partly to distract myself, I took my time with frequent stops for some creative photography, capturing this wonderland. Eventually I was able to push through my cramps, and at the first glimpse of snow drifts, I had arrived at Moiras Flats and rushed to set up my tent as dusk fell.

The catalyst for this hike was a rare weather pattern that saw an early three day dumping of snow in late autumn (May in our hemisphere). The weather forecast suggested a narrow window of five days of sunshine.
I knew I only needed three days, so off I went on a whim, with a day up my sleeve in case the weather changed. It was a calculated risk having spent a lot of time in the Australian alps. Either way, I decided to not hang around, and turned this into a single overnight hike. Moiras Flats is just inside the protection of the alpine tree line. A second night out would risk being unduly exposed to high winds up on the plateau. So, my decision was to push on and complete the hike in two days.

The last few kilometres along the ridge-line was seriously dicey, before officially joining the main defined track to the summit that starts from the Thredbo Village side. Up until now, I had spent most of the day under compass and deciphering contour lines. The snow being on the northern sunny side had started to ice over. After a heart-in-my-mouth step where I caught my slip (thanks to my hike poles), it became clear I had to bypass the next 300 metres in front of me. I deduced that I needed to get up and on top of the main ridge-line to be safe. Slightly confronting as I had to walk straight up a steep ascent for about 100 metres. "Best not to look back" (I quietly reassured myself), as I took my time to crack the ice crust with each step, and concentrate on maintaining my balance with a deliberate head down and lean into the hill.

Climbing Australia's highest mountain at 2,228 metres just before sunset at 5:25 pm, my timing was perfect in reaching the summit of Mount Kosciusko to experience the most stunning sunset of endless blue grey vista of the distant alpine mountain ranges. The view was accentuated by the white snow capped foreground of the summit walk, the main ridge, and plateau.

I knew that I would have a most wonderful moonlit walk of 11 kilometres to the (closed) chairlift at the back of the ski run, with a final two kilometre walk down the ski run to Thredbo Village.

Pausing briefly to hydrate at the chairlift and secure my head torch as I was about to enter the tree cover, I put my pack on and immediately felt that something was not quite right. It had been a very long day, and I had already covered 32 kilometres. In the short time that I had stopped, my body had seized up. My walking became stilted with my hip alignment and back tilted to one side. I thought to myself, "This is not good," but took comfort in the fact that I was in sight of the ski lodges of Thredbo Village. For what should have taken me half an hour, I ended up shuffling along for 1.5 hours, to arrive at the Alpine resort just in time before the final call for meals. When I relayed this story to my neurologist he confirmed (somewhat

disapprovingly as he looked over the top of his glasses) that I had experienced a neurological breakdown of sorts.
It had been an elapsed time of 14.5 hours, covering 34 kilometres.

*I was very excited to learn a few months later that Apple had earlier released a new feature in their Health app that captures **walking asymmetry**. Upon learning of this feature, I hurriedly scrolled back to the 23rd May 2021 and was pleased to see my average asymmetry was indeed way off the Richter scale. At 32%, it was an all time high for me, and mirrored perfectly what I had felt on that day, (with my body feeling all cockeyed to one side). For a normal abled body person, your walking asymmetry will be between zero and a couple of percentage points.*

Love technology!

With not a soul in sight, it is reasonable to think that I was the last to traverse Hannels Spur in autumn. Anyone else that might have followed this path in the ensuing days and weeks would have needed full snow-camping gear, talons, and snow shoes and/or nordic skies, which is way outside my comfort zone and experience.

Know your environment, take calculated risks, work within *your own* comfort zone, trust in yourself, and keep going!

Chapter 19
In a Pickle

A Journey to Warrnambool Pickleball Tournament

An account of four friends with Parkinson's – Feb 2024

"Hey, I've got a new sport for you, Trevor", exclaimed my neurological physiotherapist, Marize.

"It involves carbon fibre, paddles, and a gearbox". Of course I jumped at the chance, knowing full well that Marize was aware of my passion for motor racing.

I soon learnt about the awesome, exhilarating sport of Pickleball that is played with a hi-tech carbon-fibre paddle (and that Gearbox happens to be a brand of paddle). Pickleball is a hybrid game that is a mix of tennis, badminton, squash, and table tennis.

The game of Pickleball is wonderfully social, easy to learn, and suited to all age groups, and mixed ability. Played on a badminton-sized court, there are some key elements designed to keep the game close and competitive, such as: 'The Kitchen' which is a 'non-volley zone' (a line set seven feet back from the net).

The ball is made of plastic (the size of an orange) with holes in it to slow it's trajectory. Nevertheless, don't be fooled by the pace, this is a fast action game.

Since my first game in March 2023, I've become totally hooked, and can see why Pickleball is now the fastest growing sport in the world.

The national body, Pickleball Australia Association was launched in 2020. It is exciting to be involved in a sport that is in its infancy experiencing such rapid growth (the origins of the game go back to 1965 on Bainbridge Island, Washington, USA).

My home club Manningham (Doncaster East), has grown to well over 200 active members within its first year *[and 340 in our second year]*. Thanks to Marize (an innovative neurological physiotherapist), we now have nine of us with Parkinson's that have been introduced to the sport and play weekly. In fact, we now total 14 members with Parkinson's that have experienced the therapeutic benefits of playing Pickleball, beyond the social engagement and fun.

When the opportunity came up to compete at this years inaugural Warrnambool Pickleball Open, four of us 'Parky' friends (Michael, Shane, Tony, and myself) decided to catch the train down and stay at one of Warrnambool's beautiful mid century Artdeco homes, Kepler Rose.

We Parky's take sheer delight in being able to mix it up and win against normal abled competitors. With a bit of mischief in his eyes, Michael hatched a plan for he and I to play together in the men's doubles. Although we didn't get through to the finals, we had three tightly contested games.

Normally club games are played to 11. However, for this competition, we played to 15.
In our second game, Michael and I were down 5:10. After many long rallies, the score progressed to 6:12, then 9:14. Still down

and staring at defeat, Michael and I stayed calm and fought back to win at 16:14.

One of the social aspects of Pickleball is that you don't need a partner. Most clubs use an app where you register for (typically) a two-hour session and just rock up to play in a 'round-robin' game. I entered the mixed-doubles comp and ticked the box for 'need a partner'. I got to meet my allocated partner on the night before our competition, and together we teamed up and had an awesome time.

I'd mentioned to one of the event organisers Mary, that four of us with Parkinson's had registered for general events, but asked if we could have a specific mixed-ability Parkinson's event to bring about awareness of Parkinson's (and showcase how you can get on with leading an active and meaningful life no matter what). Mary was so wonderfully supportive of the idea and orchestrated a dedicated *Mixed-Ability Parkinson's* event on the Sunday, with herself and the co-organiser David pairing up with a Parky. It also meant that Roy from Ocean Grove (with Parkinson's) could team up with his wife and join in.

Pickleball is more than a game. It is about community, friendships formed, and a wonderful way to keep active.

It was a testament to the addictive nature of Pickleball that we had competitor's travel from as far afield as Queensland, South Australia, central Victoria, Melbourne, Traralgon, Drysdale, and Ocean Grove.

Special thanks goes to the organisers Mary and David, their extended team of volunteers who put on a fantastic Pickleball Warrnambool Open.

Writing is one way of staying connected to your communities of interest, whether as a participant or spectator.

Pickleball has become my primary sport playing on average twice a week in two-hour sessions. The trailing effect is amazing in the way my walking gait is greatly improved for several hours afterwards.

Such is the exciting growth of our sport, it was February 2024 that was the inaugural *Warrnambool Pickleball Tournament*. The following Thursday, I flew down to Hobart to compete for another three days in the *Tasmanian Pickleball Championships*, and if that wasn't enough, the very next week was the *Pickleball Victoria Open Championships*, back in my home state. (They have since coordinated the scheduling of these events so we don't have such a frenetic three weeks, but it was fun to gleam some small insights into what pro-level athletes go through when on tour.)

At the Victoria Open, it was an exciting achievement to receive a bronze medal for the ParaPickleball event. It has been awesome to be part of the Pickleball community, providing great camaraderie, inclusiveness that is caring and supportive without compensating for ruthlessly fun competition on the court.

At the Melbourne Convention Centre in January 2025, my home city played host for Australia's inaugural Professional Pickleball Association (PPA) tournament. It was great to be courtside, getting up close and personal with the world's best. To witness the fast-paced net rallies, the sheer power of pro-level games and athleticism was totally awe-inspiring.

Enjoy finding your tribe…

Pickleball could be your answer.

Chapter 20
The Evolving You

Your Inner Truth

As I left the Yarra Valley Living Centre, I was invited to randomly select a card of inspiration and positivity. These words have stayed with me:

> *Courage and determination*
> *are your best friends;*
> *you have faith in your ability*
> *to move forward in life.*

Draw comfort as you embrace life with the knowledge and realisation that all organisms, all matter on this Earth are in a state of impermanence.

We don't have time to concern ourselves with a future we cannot control. Practicing *mindfulness* will help us live in the present.

We are all very much *sentient beings*, all sensing, all feeling.

You are not your body.

Maintain a complete separation of mind and body. Your job is to observe your body, to nurture and protect your body with kindness and without judgement.

When was the last time you hugged yourself? Go on, give yourself a big hug now. Smile and don't forget to breathe.

When I travel, I am often asked if I am alone. My standard reply is "Solo, but never alone". We are only alone to the extent that we allow our thoughts to be.

Humanity is very much alive and well. You are not alone.

You will discover your inner truth as you find your authentic self. With total compassion, walk this planet with an open heart and you will receive kindness.

Live lightly. Take pleasure in the little things in life. You have everything you need. You have arrived, you are not waiting for anything, you are living now.

Go forth with confidence. With each foot forward, know that you are empowered to take positive steps.

You have found your balance.

South Coast Wilderness Track, Tasmania

Hannels Spur, Mt Kosciuszko

Nourish Yourself

Deconstructed Breakfast Parfait

Take delight in learning about anti-inflammatory foods. Your mitochondria will thank you.

My Nourishing Breakfast Ingredients Revealed

Have fun mixing it up beyond the ingredients I have shown below:

Ancient Grains:

Amaranth, millet, sorghum, (optional puffed rice).

Seeds:

Hemp seeds, flax (linseed), sesame seeds.

Favourite Organic Berries:

Blueberries, strawberries, raspberries.

plus:

Psyllium husk, a dash of apple cider vinegar, biodynamic yoghurt, cocoa powder, desiccated coconut (fine).

Method

The best part is there is no specific method other than the need to add water or coconut milk to mix and combine ingredients.

Enjoy experimenting with proportions and have fun throwing it all together. There are no rules but I will offer these pointers:

- I do add more of the ancient grains on the days when I know I will be more active.

- The psyllium husk is a great source of fibre. I have a slightly heaped tablespoon. You may wish to start with less if you have not been used to a high fibre diet.

- With your strawberries in particular, please try to buy organic as they are known to contain amongst the highest levels of pesticide residue. Refer: *The Environmental Working Group* https://www.ewg.org/.

- Ideally you will be able to track down the ancient puffed grains of *amaranth, millet, and sorghum*. (I have only suggested puffed rice as an option if you are unable to obtain these nourishing ancient grains).

- I use coconut yoghurt. But stick to your favourite unsweetened, natural (unflavoured) yoghurt if you prefer.

Please enjoy and I'd love to see your creations posted on instagram using the hashtag:
#natraomi_nourishingbreakfast

"Intrigo dal Cielo Oscuro"

Jazz Chart

For my dear Jazz friends,
as you settle into the calm of nocturnals,
may you feel inspired to improvise through
the *Intrigue from the Obscure Sky*

Stay Connected

Have you been inspired in someway?

My wish is that you feel empowered to continue to carve out a meaningful life despite what hurdles may present.

Stay connected and engaged in life. I would love to hear from you and share in your story.

All the very best in your journey and the evolving you.

NATRAOMI